THE ALAMO

MILESTONES
IN
AMERICAN HISTORY

MILESTONES
IN
AMERICAN HISTORY

THE ALAMO

THE BATTLE FOR TEXAS

SHANE MOUNTJOY

CHELSEA HOUSE
PUBLISHERS
An imprint of Infobase Publishing

Chelsea House
An imprint of Infobase Publishing
132 West 31st Street
New York, NY 10001

Library of Congress Cataloging-in-Publication Data

Mountjoy, Shane, 1967–
   The Alamo : the battle for Texas / Shane Mountjoy.
      p. cm. — (Milestones in American history)
   Includes bibliographical references and index.
   ISBN 978-1-60413-056-0 (hardcover)
   1. Alamo (San Antonio, Tex.)—Siege, 1836—Juvenile literature. 2. Texas—History—
Revolution, 1835–1836—Juvenile literature. I. Title. II. Series.
   F390.M855 2009
   976.4'03—dc22   2008040801

Chelsea House books are available at special discounts when purchased in bulk quantities for businesses, associations, institutions, or sales promotions. Please call our Special Sales Department in New York at (212) 967-8800 or (800) 322-8755.

You can find Chelsea House on the World Wide Web at http://www.chelseahouse.com

Series design by Erik Lindstrom
Cover design by Ben Peterson

Printed in the United States of America

Bang NMSG 10 9 8 7 6 5 4 3 2 1

This book is printed on acid-free paper.

All links and Web addresses were checked and verified to be correct at the time of publication. Because of the dynamic nature of the Web, some addresses and links may have changed since publication and may no longer be valid.

CONTENTS

Crossing the Line

Suddenly, everything became silent. The air grew still. The bark of enemy cannon no longer sounded from outside the walls. The concussion of exploding shells no longer pounded the men huddled inside the small complex. The sun slowly dropped in the sky as dusk approached. Smoke and dust saturated the parched air. William Barret Travis and nearly 200 men had managed to hold out against a constant barrage from the Mexican army for 12 days. It was late afternoon on March 5, 1836, at the Alamo in San Antonio.

Lieutenant Colonel Travis, the commanding officer of the defenders, peered over the edge of the wall. He observed the Mexican artillerymen quietly and methodically cleaning their equipment and other soldiers behind them in the Mexican lines that encircled the small compound. The opposing troops acted almost as if there were no siege.

Although somewhat inexperienced, Colonel Travis knew that the silence of the guns meant the primary attack was coming soon. He pulled out his pocket watch and looked at the sun, calculating how much daylight remained to make his preparations for the final defense of the Alamo. Enemy artillery had heavily damaged the north wall. Immediate repairs were necessary to ensure that the wall would continue to stand. There were many needs, and not enough time. Travis put his watch back into his pocket.

Looking at the faces of his men, he knew that his attitude and poise would either inspire or discourage them. A lieutenant barked out some orders to make repairs, replenish ammunition, and begin the many other basic tasks of refortifying their position. Men scurried back and forth, each on a mission to repair a hole or restock some necessary provision. The north wall received special attention, as it had suffered the brunt of the artillery shots. To fortify this position, the men piled up earth 10 feet high behind the wall. After they finished, they sat down to enjoy a meal in the break from the deafening cannon barrage.

While the men completed their tasks, Travis contemplated their situation. Although he desperately wanted to hold out until reinforcements arrived, he also realized it was unlikely that any reinforcements were coming. Several couriers had left to plead for help and each had returned without such a promise. Twice Travis had sent out his trusted friend James Bonham to request help and twice Bonham had returned empty-handed. And when he returned on March 3, Bonham brought the news that the commander at the fortress at Goliad would send no troops to relieve the Alamo. Travis and his men were on their own.

After facing their reality, Travis gave orders for every defender to assemble in the courtyard. The lieutenant colonel wanted to talk with his men. Word spread among the ranks as the young commander stood in the courtyard of the old

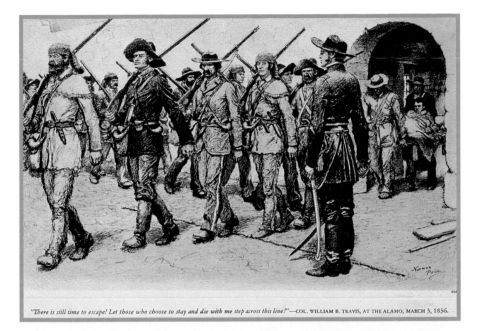

"There is still time to escape! Let those who choose to stay and die with me step across this line!"—COL. WILLIAM B. TRAVIS, AT THE ALAMO, MARCH 3, 1836.

The Battle of the Alamo is one of the most legendary military engagements in American history. A large number of personalities fought for the independence of Texas, including Davy Crockett, Jim Bowie, William Barret Travis, and Sam Houston. Pictured is a drawing of William Travis leading his military company.

Spanish mission. The exhausted defenders gathered quickly, crowding around Travis. Even the sick and wounded joined the assembly. Defenders carried those too wounded or too sick to stand, including James (Jim) Bowie. The famed knife-fighter lay on his cot in the enclosure, suffering from a high fever.

Travis cleared his throat and addressed the brave volunteers. He explained that, although help might still come, the chances of reinforcements arriving in time were slim. As he spoke, he looked men in the eyes. Some of the defenders were old, others were just teenagers. Some had fought in many battles. For others, this was their first experience of military action. Most, like Travis, were transplanted Americans, but all had come from somewhere else. Despite their differences, each of them now faced the same fate: death, not victory. If the Mexican army simply battered the walls with its cannon, the defenders would have no choice but to surrender, yet surrender offered little hope to those inside the fort. Hanging from the San Fernando Cathedral in town was a red flag, signifying that attackers would give no mercy to Travis and his men.

Travis admitted that he felt deceived. From the beginning of the siege, he had believed that help would come from outside, but it was now apparent that the Alamo defenders could expect none. They were on their own. The commander told them, "Our fate is sealed. Within this very day—perhaps within a very few hours—we must all be in eternity. This is our destiny and we cannot avoid it."[1] There was no way for the small force to escape the situation. But, Travis announced, "We must sell our lives as dearly as possible."[2]

As he spoke, the lieutenant colonel drew his sword from its scabbard. Then, he deliberately used the sword to draw a long line in the ground, from one side of the courtyard to the other. He alone stood on one side, while the attentive soldiers stood on the other. Now Travis raised his voice as he called on the defenders to choose their fate. Cross the line and stay here to face the expected onslaught or stand still and be released from all obligations to defend the stronghold. He made no attempt to shame any into staying within the fort. Instead, he expressed the desire to know who stood with him, which men he could count on in the coming battle. Each was free to make his own decision, but each needed to make that decision known now. As for the bold commander of the fort, he announced that he intended to resist "as long as there is breath in my body."[3]

When Travis finished speaking, the air again grew silent. The men stood quietly for a few seconds as they contemplated the choice before them. Then, 26-year-old Tapley Holland, an Ohio native, strode forward and crossed the line, taking his place near Travis. Others followed suit. The wounded limped and hobbled as they made their way to join their comrades across the line. Within a few moments, many of the volunteers now stood across the line with Travis. One of those still behind the line was Jim Bowie, lying on his cot. Bowie raised his voice and called to his men, "Boys, I am not able to go to you, but I wish some of you would be so kind as to remove my cot over there."[4]

Several men swiftly carried out his request. Others too sick to walk themselves asked for the same help. Only one man, Louis Rose, chose not to cross the line. Rose was a Frenchman, a veteran of Napoleon's Russian campaign. He quietly gathered his things, unable or unwilling to look the volunteers in the eye. Despite his choice, Travis and Bowie both spoke kindly to him. Later that night, when darkness enveloped the compound, Rose scaled a wall and dropped to the other side. Alone and in the dark, Rose managed to walk through the Mexican lines to safety, to freedom.

FACT OR FICTION?

Is the dramatic line-in-the-sand story true? Historians are unsure. There are many reasons to believe that the story is simply a myth. For instance, William Zuber, who had served in the Texas Volunteers, was the first to tell the story in 1873, some 37 years after the incident, and he said that Rose had given his parents the account as well. No other survivors mentioned the incident until years later. Moreover, each of the accounts varied slightly from Zuber's description. In some, the incident takes place on the first day of the siege; in others, it is three days before the Alamo fell. Regardless of when it occurred, the story illustrates the commitment of the defenders to resist the Mexican siege. There is also evidence that indicates the story is based on Ben Milam's call to action leading up to the Battle of Bexar, when Texian forces drove the Mexican army out of the Alamo in December 1835.

In some respects, however, the accuracy of the story is irrelevant. The defenders chose to stay and fight against overwhelming odds. They almost certainly knew that they faced death rather than victory. The choice to remain inside the Alamo compound and fight to the last is the important aspect of the story. That boldness, commitment, and, ultimately, that sacrifice is the real story. The line in the sand might be nothing more than a tool to tell the story. As one historian noted, "Is there any proof that Travis did not draw the line? If not, then let us believe it."[5] In any case, the anecdote lives on as an illustration of the heroic devotion the defenders inside the fort exhibited for the cause of Texas independence. Their struggle is the story of the Alamo.

Texas Before
the Alamo

The Alamo defenders struggled and died attempting to win independence for the place known as Tejas (Spanish) or Texas (English). Today, Texas is the biggest state in the continental United States, located in the south central area of the nation. In the 1830s, Texas was a large territory, but it was limited to what is now the eastern part of the state. A series of rivers flowed from the interior southeast to the Gulf of Mexico, providing natural waterways for settlements upstream. The Rio Grande, which eventually became the boundary between Texas and Mexico, was the southernmost river. The southern and western boundaries of Texas remained a source of debate until the conclusion of the Mexican-American War in 1848. Heading east and slightly north, several rivers acted as natural highways for settlers. Thus, colonists such as those recruited by Stephen F. Austin established settlements near the rivers, which included the Nueces, San Antonio, Guadalupe, Colorado, Brazos, San Jacinto, Trinity, Neches, Sabine, and Red. Austin planted the heart of his Texas colony in the east. The further one traveled west, the sparser the Anglo population became. The western landscape also became more barren, having fewer trees and less rainfall, which meant a generally parched and often hot environment.

In 1836, about 36,000 people populated the vast expanse of territory known as Texas. Of these, the largest group was approximately 17,400 from the United States, including about 2,000 blacks,[1] many of whom were slaves. Mexicans comprised only 3,600, or roughly 10 percent of the population of Texas. This presented a difficult problem for the Mexican government: There were more foreigners than Mexicans in the territory of Texas, the development of which depended upon the influx of Americans. Unfortunately, American settlers in Texas brought with them expectations of governmental institutions and rights that were consistent with the United States, but not necessarily Mexico. Civil unrest resulted in a series of Mexican governments throughout the 1820s that sought to establish control to maintain law and order. Their policies often ran counter to the expectations of American settlers in Texas. Over time, Texas settlers chose to rebel rather than submit to a government many believed to be oppressive and tyrannical. This revolt became known as the Texas Revolution.

MEXICO AT THE TIME OF THE TEXAS REVOLUTION

Mexico was hardly in a position to put down such a rebellion. The nation was young, having gained its independence from Spain in 1821. Spain had held Mexico as a colony dating back to the expeditions and conquest of the Aztecs by Hernan Cortes from 1519 to 1521. Mexican Indians never cared much for their Spanish masters. Spanish officials controlled the government, often enjoying lavish lifestyles while the people lived in dire poverty. In the three centuries of Spanish rule, many Mexicans suffered as slaves, and Spain seized the riches

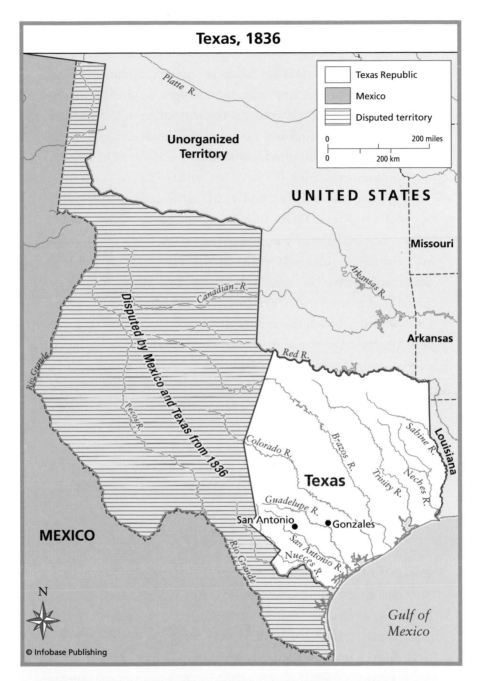

Texas, 1836

| Texas Republic |
| Mexico |
| Disputed territory |

0   200 miles
0   200 km

Platte R.

Unorganized Territory

UNITED STATES

Missouri

Canadian R.

Disputed by Mexico and Texas from 1836

Arkansas R.

Rio Grande

Pecos R.

Red R.

Arkansas

Colorado R.

Brazos R.

Sabine R.

Louisiana

Trinity R.

Neches R.

Texas

Guadelupe R.

San Antonio   Gonzales

MEXICO

Rio Grande

San Antonio R.

Nueces R.

N

Gulf of Mexico

© Infobase Publishing

Spain was the first European nation to make claims on Texas. It was then governed by Mexico, from 1821 to 1836, until it became the independent Republic of Texas. In 1845, Texas became the twenty-eighth state of the United States.

of Mexico for itself. The successful fight against Spanish rule began in 1810 when Miguel Hidalgo y Costilla, a Catholic priest, determined to take a stand against Spain. Hidalgo insisted that Spain end taxation and slavery. Spanish authorities took steps to put down the revolt, capturing and executing Hidalgo in 1811. His death, however, did not end the struggle. Indeed, now the movement had a martyr, and the fight continued for another decade.

Fighting raged for several years, with neither side gaining the advantage. Spain had the resources to field a large, well-equipped professional army. The rebels engaged in guerrilla warfare, with small bands of fighters inflicting damage and casualties on the Spaniards whenever and wherever they could. The pivotal moment came in 1820 when a Spanish general switched sides in the conflict. General Agustin de Iturbide had fought in the Spanish army in Mexico throughout much of the conflict, rising from lieutenant in 1810 to general in 1816. Over time, however, Iturbide became increasingly sympathetic to the Mexican cause. He opened secret negotiations with the rebels and then openly joined the revolt in 1820. Most of his troops followed their general, giving the fight for Mexican independence a much-needed army. Iturbide led the rebels to victory and Mexico gained its independence from Spain.

Like many countries born of successful rebellions, Mexico struggled after achieving autonomy. The Mexican Congress named Iturbide emperor, bestowing the title Augustus I on him. The career soldier did not fare well leading a government. The experiences of leading an army at war—issuing orders and punishing those who questioned orders—created enemies. Growing resentment led to his abdication in a military coup in 1823. Mexico established a republic in 1824, adopting a constitution that closely resembled the United States Constitution. Still, no leader emerged with enough support or ability to unite the country, which resulted in lingering unrest. A succession of military leaders seized power until General Antonio Lopez de Santa Anna proclaimed himself the president of Mexico in 1833. Santa Anna chose to ignore the constitution when it suited him, leading to friction with Texian residents, many of whom had come from the United States.

The presence of so many Americans in Texas was sure to lead to problems for Mexican rule over the territory. French visitor Alexis de Tocqueville traveled throughout America a few years before the Texas Revolution, recording many of his observations. Fittingly, he foresaw that although Mexico controlled Texas, the makeup of Texas would lead to its eventual inclusion into the United States. De Tocqueville observed:

> The lands of the New World belong to the first occupant; and they are the natural reward of the swiftest pioneer. Even the countries which are already peopled will have some difficulty in securing themselves from this invasion. I have already alluded to what is taking place in the province of Texas. The inhabitants of the United States are perpetually migrating to Texas, where they purchase land; and although they conform to the laws of the country, they are gradually founding the empire of their own language and their own manners. The province of Texas is still part of the Mexican dominions, but it will soon contain no Mexicans; the same thing has occurred whenever the Anglo-Americans have come into contact with populations of a different origin.[2]

As de Tocqueville correctly predicted, the settlement of Americans into Texas effectively guaranteed that Texas would become more American than Mexican. Government institutions and practices in Texas more resembled American institutions than those found in Mexico did. Accordingly, the United States more easily assimilated Texians into its nation than Mexico assimilated those transplanted Americans into its nation.

THE AUSTINS

Encouraging Americans to settle in Texas was a relatively new approach to colonizing the region. While Spanish authorities controlled Mexico, they refused to permit Anglos to settle in Texas. However, an obscure American concluded that Texas offered opportunities for his future and that Mexican independence offered the prospect that policies prohibiting Anglo settlement might be altered. This man, Moses Austin, a resident of Missouri, decided to travel to Mexico and talk with authorities about establishing colonies of Americans in Texas. In 1820, Austin left for San Antonio de Bexar, where he managed to receive a land grant in what is now Texas. This grant named him the *empresario*, or person granted the right to establish a settlement in Spanish territory. The grant also required the empresario to recruit settlers and lead the settlement. Austin became the first Anglo named empresario. After securing the grant, Austin headed home to begin recruiting colonists to populate his settlement. On his return trip to Missouri in January 1821, thieves attacked and beat him. Weakened and disheartened, Austin managed to make it back home, but soon fell gravely ill. Before he died, he bequeathed his grant to his son, Stephen.

Upon inheriting the land grant, Stephen Fuller Austin put his deceased father's affairs in order, gathered the necessary

(opposite) **Stephen Fuller Austin (1793–1836), also known as the "Father of Texas," led the successful colonization of the region by American settlers. He was responsible for bringing 1,200 American families into Mexican Texas. Although Austin believed that an alliance between American colonists and Mexican officials was the best way to solve disputes, he later took command of an attack on Mexican troops in San Antonio.**

supplies and some men, and then headed west to San Antonio in mid-August 1821. Austin intended to approach Mexican officials and obtain approval to implement his father's land grant. On the way, word reached the band that Mexico had declared its independence from Spain. Texas no longer belonged to Spain—it now belonged to Mexico. When Austin arrived in San Antonio, Mexican officials reauthorized the land grant. Austin immediately began recruiting more individuals and families to move to his large parcel of Texas land. A family of four could receive 1,280 acres for 12.5 cents an acre. Austin's first settlers arrived at the colony in what is now Fort Bend County, Texas, on the Brazos River, in December 1821.

Mexico's independence muddied Austin's plans. After the first settlers had already arrived, the new government of Mexico voided all Spanish land grants, which meant that Austin and his colonists were occupying Mexican land illegally. Austin went to Mexico City and pleaded his case. In January 1821, the Mexican government agreed to recognize the Austin grant, as well as recognizing Austin as empresario, or a government agent to promote immigration. Serving as the official government representative entitled Austin to claim 67,000 acres of land for every 200 families he settled in Texas.

Soon, Austin faced another hurdle. In March 1823, Iturbide I abdicated his throne. The new government rescinded the law that recognized Austin's grant. Seeking to restore the grant, Austin agreed to recruit an additional 100 families to Texas, which would satisfy his obligations. By the end of 1825, having already relocated 300 families to Texas, Austin received permission to recruit another 900 families. As the empresario, Austin had both civil and military authority over the residents in his settlement. He established legal institutions and practices that resembled the American legal system and even created a constitution to govern the colony. Austin arranged for protection by organizing small groups of men, the beginnings of the Texas Rangers. He soon discovered that the costs of providing governmental services prevented him from making a profit.

THE MEXICAN CONSTITUTION OF 1824

About a year and a half after Iturbide relinquished power, Mexico adopted a new constitution. The so-called Constitution of 1824 created a republic in which elected representatives ran the government. Framers copied several basic elements of the U.S. Constitution. For instance, the new government included a bicameral legislature with upper and lower houses. The upper house, or Senate, allowed each state to elect two senators; the lower house, or Chamber of Deputies, was based upon population—the larger the state, the more deputies. The new constitution also provided for the election of a president and vice president, with each serving four-year terms. Also like the United States, the Mexican government had a federal Supreme Court. The states and national government shared power. The constitution even called the new republic the United Mexican States, comprised of 19 free and independent states along with 5 territories. The 1824 Constitution integrated Texas into the Mexican state of Coahuila. Thus, Texas at the time of the revolution was Coahuila y Tejas.

Despite the similarities, there were also several distinct differences between the U.S. Constitution and the Mexican Constitution of 1824. The most significant of these differences involved religion. The new republic had a state religion, the Roman Catholic Church. By law, all citizens were required to tithe—that is, pay 10 percent of their income as a gift—to the state church. Local officials collected the tithes, but Anglo settlers, especially Americans, disliked this requirement.

American settlers to Texas generally accepted the 1824 document, despite some of its objectionable attributes. Overall, the constitution placed few restrictions on individual freedom. Thus, many transplants to Texas had no trouble swearing allegiance to the Mexican government established by the

D. ANTONIO LOPEZ DE SANTA ANNA,

General de Division,

varias veces Presidente de la República Mejicana.

Antonio Lopez de Santa Anna (1794–1876) started his long military career at the age of 16. In 1833, he became president of Mexico, but the nation soon deteriorated into chaos. His less democratic form of rule eventually led to dissatisfaction with the Mexican government, sparking the Texas Revolution.

republican constitution. The inclusion of "1824" on the Alamo flag demonstrates the partiality American settlers felt for the constitution. After Santa Anna seized power in April 1834, however, the headstrong ruler took steps that undermined the republic.

UNREST

In early 1835, Santa Anna began to demonstrate tyrannical tendencies—for example, he removed officials who opposed his policies, dissolved state legislatures, and set up a national legislature that he controlled. With power consolidated, Santa Anna set about weakening the federal structure of the 1824 constitution and strengthening the power of the federal government. Texians watched nervously as the process continued to limit local powers until Mexico City merged Texas into the state of Coahuila. This merger weakened Texian influence on decisions affecting Texas. Specifically, the central government in Mexico City set all taxes on Texas without giving the residents appropriate representation in the federal government. Mexico City uncovered widespread land-fraud involving the Coahuila governor and members of the state legislature. In June 1835, Santa Anna moved quickly to end the corruption, declaring martial law in Saltillo, the capital of Coahuila. Some Texians responded to this action by joining the War Party, a group advocating independence from Mexico.

Santa Anna's actions did little to instill confidence in Texians who favored a republican form of government. On October 3, 1835, Santa Anna forced the revocation of the Constitution of 1824. A new government was established that placed far more power in the hands of the central government. Under the new government, Santa Anna became dictator.

Texas responded by holding a convention, the Texas Consultation of Delegates, to chart its course. The delegates opened the session on October 16, 1835, in San Felipe. The group wanted to establish a temporary government, but fighting at the siege and battle of San Antonio that fall drew several delegates away from the proceedings. The delegates reassembled on November 3 with the necessary quorum to conduct business. After debating for three days, the convention approved a resolution whereby the Texians resolved to fight for the restoration

SANTA ANNA
(1794–1876)

"The Napoleon of the West"

Born in 1794 in the city of Vera Cruz, Antonio Lopez de Santa Anna grew up to become the undisputed foe of Texas in the nineteenth century. Usually known as Santa Anna, the future dictator was trained in the Spanish army where he rose quickly through the ranks. He was one of the key army leaders who turned against Spain and fought for Mexican independence, which was achieved in 1821. Santa Anna first held the presidency in 1833. His autocratic style of leadership led to the Texas Revolution in 1835–1836. Not content to allow others to lead the army, the president commanded the Mexican troops that laid siege to the Alamo in 1836. The self-styled "Napoleon of the West" ordered that no prisoners be taken when his troops overwhelmed the Alamo defenders. Flush with the victory, Santa Anna pursued the main Texian force across Texas until an army led by Sam Houston defeated the Mexican president and general at the Battle of San Jacinto. When presented to Houston, Santa Anna reportedly said, "That man may consider himself born to no common destiny who has conquered the Napoleon of the West."*

Following the loss of Texas, Santa Anna managed to regain power and lose another war, this time to the United States in the Mexican-American War of 1846–1848. The war with the United States began of the 1824 Mexican Constitution. This resolution, announced the next day, became known as the Declaration of November 7, 1835. The convention then established the Texas Provisional Government to run their affairs in the interim. The provisional government created the Texas Revolutionary Army and named Sam Houston the commander of all its forces, with the

over a disputed boundary of Texas, which the United States had annexed in 1845. In between the two conflicts over Texas, Santa Anna served his country when he fought against a French attack at Vera Cruz in 1842. After a cannonball shattered his ankle, which led to the amputation of his leg, Santa Anna buried the leg with full military honors. Then, the one-legged hero reminded his fellow citizens of the personal sacrifice he had made to demonstrate his commitment to Mexico. Even though the French forced Mexico to accept their demands, Santa Anna returned to Mexican politics a hero.

The "Napoleon of the West" exhibited the rare ability to work his way into the inner circle of Mexican power. Moreover, he managed this feat repeatedly. Over the course of 22 years, Santa Anna held the office of President of Mexico 11 different times. Much like the real Napoleon, Santa Anna never really left the public eye. His political return always seemed possible. Following his removal from power in the mid-1850s, Santa Anna lived in exile until he was granted amnesty and returned to Mexico City in 1874. He died two years later at the age of 82, a broken old man lacking money and friends. Death had finally conquered the "Napoleon of the West."

*Edwin P. Hoyt, The Alamo: An Illustrated History. *Dallas: Taylor Publishing Company, 1999, 167–168.*

exception of those men fighting at San Antonio. The delegates decided to reconvene on March 1, 1836, and then adjourned. By the time the convention met again, the two sides would have engaged in three battles and a Mexican army would be laying siege to volunteers at the Alamo.

The Seeds
of Revolution

The turmoil facing Mexico in the 1830s over its renegade
province was a symptom of something much larger than
Texas—a very powerful force driven by idealism, which was
known as Manifest Destiny. Americans in the nineteenth century believed themselves to be the inheritors of special God-
given privileges and responsibilities. Some of these privileges
and responsibilities included conquering the North American
continent. Manifest Destiny "meant expansion, prearranged
by Heaven, over an area not clearly defined."[1] Some viewed
Manifest Destiny as the United States claiming land westward
to the Pacific Ocean. Others expanded the idea to include all
of North America and sometimes the entire Western Hemi-
sphere. In spite of the various extensions or limitations of
the vision, Manifest Destiny stimulated western settlement
and later, an upheaval in American politics in the 1840s. The

Emanuel Leutze's *Westward the Course of Empire Takes Its Way* depicts the idea of Manifest Destiny. The pioneers, wagons, guides, and their mules are traveling on a divinely ordained pilgrimage to the Promised Land of the western frontier. It was believed that America had been chosen for the task of expanding westward, to drive out the wilderness and establish civilization.

principles of expansion captured the imagination of the young nation, leading to an unfortunate Indian policy that effectively obliterated Native American cultures.

The United States did not fully feel the effects of Manifest Destiny until the 1840s, but its seeds were already sprouting in the 1830s, evidenced by Indian wars, the growth of American nationalism, and the spread of settlers to the West. Although expansion into Texas was not a formal part of American policy, Americans did most of the colonizing there. Indeed, the United States stood to benefit from the growth of an American population in Texas. After all, the creation of a friendly neighboring state would allow more Americans to migrate west; moreover, such a territory might eventually desire to join the United States. Since the result would no doubt include the expansion of American influence or territory, American population growth in Texas helped advance the notion of Manifest Destiny.

There is one key element of Manifest Destiny—namely racial superiority—that is noticeably absent in 1830s Texas. Although transplanted Americans railed against the Mexican government, they did so for political and ideological reasons, in support of liberty and against tyranny. Texian leaders complained about the loss of individual and property rights, objected to the abuses of the centralized government, and advocated civil liberties. Such talk is not the language of those claiming superiority but the expression of individuals fighting for something much larger than themselves. In the case of Texas, the seeds of Manifest Destiny are rooted in the American ideals of freedom, independence, self-governance, and individual rights. Although Stephen F. Austin may not have initially intended it, his colonists brought with them "the special virtues of the American people and their institutions; their mission to redeem and remake the world in the image of America; and the American destiny under God to accomplish this sublime task."[2] Understandably, the influx of such ideals alarmed Mexican officials such as Santa Anna.

THE ADAMS-ONÍS TREATY

Before Mexico became independent, Spain also seemed to fear American expansion at its expense. Following the temporary loss of Spanish Florida to the United States during the War of 1812, the declining European power set out to shore up its North American holdings. The United States did not mask its intentions to gobble up Florida. Secretary of State John Quincy Adams told his Spanish counterpart, Luis de Onís, that Spain must take steps to secure "the protection of her territory" or "cede to the United States a province of which she retains nothing but the nominal possession."[3] Spain needed either to increase expenditures to protect Florida or give up the province to the United States.

At first, Spain resisted ceding control of Florida to the United States. The American delegation insisted on obtaining Florida and also demanded that Spain recognize American western land claims as extending to the Pacific Ocean. This, too, Spain opposed. Nevertheless, the treaty negotiations in 1819 offered Spain the opportunity to address one of its more pressing concerns: Texas. Spain agreed to give up Florida to the United States, and, in return, the United States recognized all Spanish claims west of the Sabine River, specifically Texas. Under the terms of the Adams-Onís Treaty, the United States renounced all claims to Texas, while Spain recognized U.S. claims to the Pacific Northwest.

For all its efforts, Spain failed to retain its colonies in the Americas, losing many of them during the 1810s and 1820s. Successful revolts dislodged the Spanish in Paraguay (1811), Uruguay (1815), Argentina (1816), Chile (1818), Peru (1821), the rest of Central America (1821), and what later became Venezuela, Colombia, and Panama (1825). While Spain fought to maintain control over its widespread empire, Mexico fought for its independence beginning in 1810, winning autonomy in 1821. Spain managed to hang on to Puerto Rico and Cuba, both island colonies. Under such conditions, the terms of the Adams-Onís Treaty of 1819, agreed to by Spain, ended up protecting Mexican claims to western lands, including Texas. Nonetheless, attempts to form stable governments in Mexico failed, allowing Americans to increase their population in Texas. The presence of Americans in the Mexican province resulted in the expansion of American influence, as the newly transplanted settlers brought with them many of their U.S. institutions, expectations, and attitudes.

In 1822, after ratifying the Adams-Onís Treaty, the United States recognized Argentina, Chile, Colombia, and Mexico as independent and self-governing nations. The Spanish empire in the New World ended, while the attainment of an American empire began to gain ground. This new empire, founded upon the principles and ideals of Manifest Destiny, was to have profound consequences for the future of Texas.

"THE LEXINGTON OF TEXAS"

The results of American attitudes soon surfaced in the town of Gonzales in 1835. The citizenry there held a cannon belonging to the Mexican garrison stationed in San Antonio. The brass-bound gun was an old, six-pound artillery piece that had first arrived in 1831. Although functional, the cannon was more a showpiece than a military tool. In 1813, during the Mexican fight for independence, the Republican army captured and spiked the gun, making it necessary to light each shell by means of a wick running the length of the barrel. On occasion, Gonzales officials fired the cannon to warn settlers when native Indians were in the area. Otherwise, the cannon remained silent, perched atop the Gonzales fort as an incentive to local Indians to keep the peace. In short, the cannon posed no serious threat to anyone.

Rising tensions and the mandate to disarm Texians, however, changed the Mexican view of the Gonzales artillery piece. Colonel Ugartechea, commander of Mexican forces in San Antonio, sent word to Gonzales from Fort Velasco demanding the return of the cannon. Ugartechea insisted that San Antonio needed it for its defense. Civic leaders in Gonzales did not take the request seriously. After all, the garrison in San Antonio not only had many more guns, but those it had were much larger than and superior to the small weapon sitting in their fort. Andrew Ponton, the mayor of Gonzales, polled the residents and discovered almost unanimous resistance to turning over the cannon to the Mexican army. Colonists took the cannon to a peach orchard where they buried it. Then the citizenry prepared for a possible confrontation and sent word to Ugarte-chea, refusing to hand over the cannon.

Colonel Ugartechea responded by dispatching 100 dragoons under Lieutenant Francisco Castaneda to reclaim the cannon. Reaching the Guadalupe River near Gonzales, Castaneda found the river too high to cross. On the opposite bank, 18 Texians prepared to resist the Mexican force. Castaneda decided to wait for the water level to drop and set up camp. The Texians buried the cannon and called for volunteers to join their cause. Two militias responded and the force retrieved the cannon and mounted it on a cart. The Texians now had a moveable artillery gun and 140 men to oppose Castaneda.

The Texians set out on the evening of October 1, 1835. They reached the Mexican camp at 3:00 A.M. A short gunfight ensued, but neither side suffered any casualties. When daylight came, the two sides entered into negotiations. Castaneda expressed understanding for the Texians, who in turn called on him to join the rebellion. Stunned at the Texian brashness, Castaneda ended all talks.

The Texians returned to their lines and produced a rudimentary battle flag depicting the cannon in question and the words "Come and take it." Lacking cannon balls, the Texians filled their cannon with scrap metal, firing the ad hoc artillery at the Mexican troops. Then the rebels fired their rifles and charged at the soldiers. Instead of fighting, Castaneda chose to return to San Antonio empty-handed. Despite the lack of bloodshed in the first clash, the Texan Revolution had begun. Future battles would include far more casualties than this initial skirmish.

THE BATTLE OF CONCEPCIÓN

When Castaneda returned to San Antonio in early October, he and his detachment rejoined the Mexican forces there. Santa Anna's revocation of the Constitution of 1824 led other

Mexican states to revolt. Mexico City recalled many of the troops from San Antonio to help put down these other uprisings. The approximately 650 soldiers left in San Antonio were cut off from the rest of Mexico. Texas was now in open revolt and General Martín Perfecto de Cos faced the prospect of fighting a rebel army with his poorly trained force largely made up of convicts. Cos also lacked enough supplies and equipment to hold out for very long.

Meanwhile, the volunteers at Gonzales selected Stephen F. Austin to serve as their general on October 11. Calling themselves the Army of Texas, the rebel forces left for San Antonio. On the way, other volunteers led by Captain Ben Milam joined their column. An advance party engaged a small detachment of mounted dragoons on October 15, resulting in a firefight. The Texians pursued the Mexican party all the way to San Antonio. Austin and the main body of his force reached San Antonio on October 19.

Assessing the situation, Austin decided to lay siege to San Antonio. He sent out a scouting party under American pioneer and soldier Jim Bowie to search the area for an appropriate place from which to conduct operations and to return by nightfall. Bowie and his group of 90 men took most of the day to locate the Mission Concepción and, deciding not to return, made camp for the night. General Cos learned that Austin's force was divided and led his own force of 400 Mexicans and two cannon against Bowie's party.

Cos and his troops advanced in the midst of a heavy fog on October 28, 1836. A small skirmish briefly ensued, but the main engagement only began when the fog lifted. The battle went poorly for Cos and his soldiers who had inferior firearms and gunpowder. The Mexicans were equipped with muskets that had a range of only 75 yards compared with the Texian rifles' range of 200 yards, and the deficiencies in the gunpowder meant a lack of firepower, which caused the musket balls to fall short or do little damage. The Texians hid themselves among

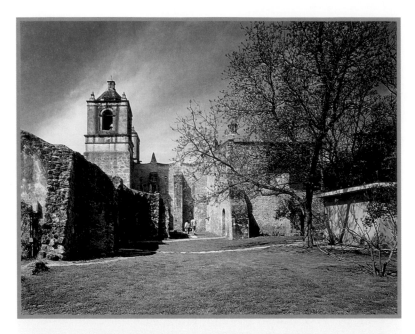

The first major engagement of the Texas Revolution was fought on the grounds of the Mission Concepción (*above*), two miles from San Antonio de Bexar. Although the Texian army was vastly outnumbered, they were able to repel several attacks by the Mexican army until the remainder of the Texian army arrived. Only one Texian soldier was killed while 76 Mexican soldiers died or were wounded.

trees and thick brush in a ravine, effectively shielding themselves from Mexican grapeshot. Texian snipers killed those manning Mexican artillery, forcing Cos and his men to retreat. The Texians then charged, wheeled around the unattended cannon, turning them on the Mexicans and driving them from the field. Austin and the remaining Texian army arrived as the battle ended. Mounted Texians pursued the Mexicans as they fled for the safety of San Antonio. The Texians lost just one man in the Battle of Concepción while the Mexicans suffered 76 killed or wounded.

THE BATTLE OF BEXAR

While Texian political leaders gathered and made plans to protect their rights under the Mexican Constitution of 1824, Texian military units made efforts to win their rights on the field of battle. A large Mexican force had occupied Bexar, the Spanish name for San Antonio, since the summer of 1835. Santa Anna sent his brother-in-law, General Martín Perfecto de Cos, to deal with rebellious Americans living in the area. The sudden presence of so many Mexican troops in Bexar heightened fears that Mexico City intended to force submission to the new government. In mid-October, Stephen F. Austin led 300 men out of Gonzales to drive the Mexicans from San Antonio. Another force under James Bowie established a perimeter around San Antonio at the end of the same month, but waited for more troops before attacking. The Texians settled in for a lengthy siege of Bexar.

The Texians were unprepared for siege life. Many volunteers found it too boring to stay and returned home. General Edward Burleson took command of the Texians on November 24. He inherited a force that suffered from dwindling supplies and low morale. The worst of winter was looming, causing Burleson to weigh ending the siege and pulling back into winter quarters. Some of Burleson's staff rejected this idea and argued for an assault on the Alamo. Many of the volunteers wanted to attack. The officers and men won out and the Texian force remained. Colonel Ben Milam challenged the Texians, appealing to their valor. Milam reportedly asked, "Who will go with old Ben Milam into San Antonio?" Three hundred Texians said they were ready to fight.

On December 5, the Texians attacked. Slowly, the assault dislodged Mexican defenders, one house at a time. On December 7, the attackers gained more ground, but lost Ben Milam, who died in the fighting. The Texians advanced far enough into the city that Cos was forced to move his headquarters to the Alamo. A relief column of 600 men arrived on the afternoon of December 8, but it was comprised of untrained, worn-out, and hungry men, most of whom were convicts who had been pressed into military service. The reinforcements rose up against their officers in a potential mutiny. After quelling the disturbance, Cos still faced the threat of the advancing rebels.

The Mexican general considered the situation. His troops could not fight their way out into the open country because they would be cut off from their supplies and exposed to Texian cavalry. They could abandon the city and withdraw to the Alamo, "but the mission-turned-garrison was already crowded with troops and refugees from the city."[4] The reinforcements only complicated the situation since most of them lacked even minimal training and would be useless in defending against a siege. The 600 extra men also taxed a dwindling supply of food. Cos realized that Texian artillery could simply pound the walls of the Alamo into rubble.

Early in the morning of December 9, General Cos assembled his staff. He received the latest updates and then explained the situation. After receiving input from his officers, Cos decided to sue for peace. The Mexicans sent a small delegation under the protection of a white flag to meet with General Burleson. Negotiations between the two sides lasted all day, finally ending at two o'clock in the morning. The two leaders met and signed the agreement at 10:00 A.M. on December 10, 1835. The siege and battle for Bexar ended. Under the terms of the surrender, Cos and his men were allowed to return to Mexico after taking an oath never again to fight against Texians "or to interfere with the restoration of the Mexican Constitution of 1824."[5] Three days later, General Martín Perfecto de Cos led about 1,100 Mexican soldiers out of the city to Mexico.

The task of maintaining a city proved easier than maintaining a force to hold the city. Within a few weeks, the volunteers disbanded and the soldiers returned to their homes. The task of holding the Alamo fell to James C. Neill.

Lieutenant Colonel James Clinton Neill commanded the garrison at the Alamo before the siege began. A native of North Carolina, Neill had migrated from Alabama to Texas in 1831 with his wife and their three children. General Sam Houston placed Neill in charge of the Alamo at the end of December 1835. However, an ill-conceived plan to attack the Mexican port city of Matamoros drained the Alamo defenses of men, munitions, food, and even clothing. When Neill assumed command, only 80 soldiers remained in the Alamo garrison. Jim Bowie was there commanding the volunteers, while Neill commanded the regulars. Both Bowie and Neill believed that the mission compound was defensible and strategically important to the Texian cause.

Nonetheless, Houston ordered the Alamo destroyed in mid-January, a move opposed by both commanders there. Bowie sent a dispatch to Houston: "Colonel Neill and myself have come to the solemn resolution that we will rather die in these ditches than give it up to the enemy."[6] Bowie also framed the issue in terms of protecting the local inhabitants from Mexican troops: "The citizens deserve our protection and the public safety demands our lives rather than to evacuate this post to the enemy."[7]

Travis, who resented his posting to San Antonio, agreed with Bowie. Once he arrived at the Alamo, he echoed many of the same sentiments Bowie had previously expressed to Houston:

> This being the Frontier Post nearest the Rio Grande, will be the first to be attacked. We are illy [sic] prepared for their organized state—Yet we are determined to sustain it as long as there is a man left; because we consider death preferable to disgrace, which would be the result of giving up a Post which has been so dearly won, and thus opening the door for the Invaders to enter the sacred Territory of the colonies.[8]

Santa Anna certainly understood the value of San Antonio de Bexar, stating that "he who controls Goliad and Bexar has Texas in the palm of his hand."[9] The Mexican general moved northward leading a large army to secure those two key points.

Bowie, Neill, and Travis seemingly agreed on little besides the importance of defending the Alamo. Moreover, not only did each believe himself more capable than the other two, each claimed the authority to command the garrison. All the while and unbeknownst to the squabbling colonels, a large Mexican army with an unquestioned leader approached. Evidently, Neill, tired of the bickering, requested a furlough to care for his sick family and received it. He left the Alamo on February 13, 1836, and did not return in time to participate in the battle. After Neill left, the two remaining colonels jockeyed for power.

Later, Travis wrote that the Alamo "is the key to Texas and should not be neglected by the Govt."[10] Ignoring the commanders' views of the looming threat, however, Sam Houston and the provisional government neglected the Alamo. "Houston appears to have been blind to the strategic importance of San Antonio."[11] Bexar acted as the gateway to the Anglo colonies of Texas. San Antonio was situated west of the important settlements of Gonzales, Columbus, and San Felipe. Besides its western location, San Antonio also served as the crossroads from Mexico to the Anglo colonies lying to the east and on the coast. The roads to each of these communities flowed from San Antonio. Whoever held San Antonio also controlled the supply and communication lines from Mexico to the Anglo settlements.

Perhaps Bowie and Travis overstated their case, yet the simple fact remains that the small outpost of San Antonio was strategically important. Apparently, Houston failed to grasp this, which might explain his reluctance to reinforce the settlement. Another possibility is that Houston wanted to abandon the fort and never truly agreed with the decision to hold the Alamo.

(continues on page 36)

Sam Houston (1793–1863), the son of a Revolutionary War soldier, was a politician and the commander in chief of the Texian army. Although he kept up a retreat from the Mexican army for over a month, eventually his attack of Santa Anna's forces at San Jacinto led to the independence of Texas in 1836.

THE TEXAS DECLARATION OF INDEPENDENCE

The Convention of 1836 began meeting on March 1 to discuss a declaration of independence. Santa Anna and his army had been besieging the Alamo since February 23. The delegates understood the need for swift action. As soon as the convention opened, the participants appointed five members to serve as a committee to draft the document proclaiming the independence of Texas. This small group—comprised of George C. Childress, Edward Conrad, James Gaines, Bailey Hardeman, and Collin McKinney—immediately began its important task. Most historians believe that Childress, who chaired the committee, was the primary author of the document. Since the committee presented a completed declaration to the full convention the following day, it is likely that Childress had already prepared a draft of the document prior to the convention. The convention approved the Texas Declaration of Independence on March 2, 1836.

The document closely follows the United States Declaration of Independence by listing reasons for independence. Sixty men signed the manuscript. The Texas document included reasons such as the preservation of rights and the abuse of powers by the Mexican government. Here is a portion of this vital document:

When a government has ceased to protect the lives, liberty and property of the people, from whom its legitimate powers are derived, and for the advancement of whose happiness it was instituted, and so far from being a guarantee for the enjoyment of those inestimable and inalienable rights, becomes an instrument in the hands of evil rulers for their oppression.

When the Federal Republican Constitution of their country, which they have sworn to support, no longer has a substantial existence, and the whole nature of their government has been forcibly changed, without their consent, from a restricted federative republic, composed of sovereign states, to a consolidated central military despotism, in which every interest is disregarded but that of the army and the priesthood, both the eternal enemies of civil liberty, the ever-ready minions of power, and the usual instruments of tyrants.

When, long after the spirit of the constitution has departed, moderation is at length so far lost by those in power, that even the semblance of freedom is removed, and the forms themselves of the constitution discontinued, and so far from their petitions and remonstrances being regarded, the agents who bear them are thrown into dungeons, and mercenary armies sent forth to force a new government upon them at the point of the bayonet.

When, in consequence of such acts of malfeasance and abdication on the part of the government, anarchy prevails, and civil society is dissolved into its original elements. In such a crisis, the first law of nature, the right of self-preservation, the inherent and inalienable rights of the people to appeal to first principles, and take their political affairs into their own hands in extreme cases, enjoins it as a right towards themselves, and a sacred obligation to their posterity, to abolish such government, and create another in its stead, calculated to rescue them from impending dangers, and to secure their future welfare and happiness.*

---

*Texas State Library and Archives Commission. Available online at http://www.tsl.state.tx.us./treasures/republic/declare-01.html/.

(continued from page 32)

Houston, writing later of the Alamo and Goliad commanders, said that "their policy of warfare was to divide, advance, and conquer. My policy was to concentrate, retreat, and conquer."[12] Whatever his reasons, Houston's lethargic actions cost the Alamo defenders dearly.

Bowie, Travis,
and Crockett

The defenders of the Alamo came from various backgrounds and included many ordinary men. The siege and battle made all of the defenders martyrs and heroes. Nevertheless, three of the defenders came to symbolize the struggle at the Alamo: Jim Bowie, William Barret Travis, and David (Davy) Crockett. Each is an easily recognized name and icon in American history, especially in Texas. Of the three, Travis was unknown before his role in the Battle of the Alamo. However, both Bowie and Crockett were well known prior to the Alamo siege. The presence of two celebrated Americans added to Texian and American shock when reports told of the slaughter. The story of each of these three men also represents those of the defenders, each of whom traveled to Texas in search of a better life.

JIM BOWIE

Jim Bowie was the ninth of ten children born to Rezin and Elve Bowie in Logan County, Kentucky, on April 10, 1796. Bowie's father fought in the Revolutionary War where he sustained injuries. In 1782, Rezin married the nurse who cared for him as he recovered from his wounds. The Bowies moved often and young Jim lived in Kentucky, Missouri, and Louisiana. He grew up accustomed to life on the frontier, becoming skilled at fighting, hunting, fishing, and surviving. Many knew Bowie as daring and courageous. While developing his skills, the young boy also received an education. Not only could Bowie read and write in English, Spanish, and French, he also spoke all three languages fluently.

In late 1814, Bowie enlisted in the Louisiana militia to fight the British in the War of 1812. He and his brother were in a unit that arrived at New Orleans after the final battle of that war had ended. The militia discharged Bowie, who then went to Rapides Parish where he sawed timber for a living. Ever the adventurer, in 1819 Bowie joined up with an expedition of American mercenaries seeking to help Mexico gain its independence from Spain and redraw the Louisiana boundary to include Texian territory. Initially, the expedition was a success, but Bowie returned to Louisiana before Spanish forces drove the party out of Texas.

Slave Trader and Land Speculator

After returning from Louisiana, Bowie sought ways to make his fortune through land speculation, buying land and selling it for more than the original purchase price. In order to buy land, Bowie needed cash, and to acquire the cash, he devised a scheme that took advantage of existing slave-trading laws. The United States government had prohibited the importation of slaves in 1808. Many southern states, to deter importing slaves and comply with federal prohibitions, used informants to learn

Jim Bowie (1796–1836) had a reputation for being bold and fearless. He took part in many adventures and was a friend to the American Indians. He was a leader of the Texas militia at the Battle of Concepción and the Battle of the Alamo.

about the slave trade, seized slaves based on this information, and sold them at public auction. The informants then received half the selling price as a reward for their service to the state. Bowie made a mockery of this system when on three separate occasions he traveled to Galveston Island and received slaves from his business partner, a famous pirate named Jean Lafitte. Bowie then smuggled the slaves into Louisiana, only to take them to the customhouse and turn himself in. Then, he bought the slaves at auction, but received one-half the selling price back as a reward for informing on himself! Since Bowie had legally purchased the slaves at public auction, he was now free to transport and sell them in any U.S. state or territory that allowed slavery. Bowie and his brother Rezin carried on the scheme until they had acquired enough money for their plans to speculate on land.

In 1825, Bowie and two of his brothers purchased a plantation near Alexandria, Louisiana, called Acadia. The Bowies constructed a steam mill to grind sugarcane, the first in Louisiana. Many viewed Acadia as the ideal plantation, yet the Bowies sold the property and 65 slaves in 1831. With this revenue, the brothers purchased a plantation in Arkansas.

Due to their land speculation, Bowie and another brother, John, were also involved in a key court dispute in the latter part of the 1820s. When Thomas Jefferson purchased the Louisiana Territory in 1803, the U.S. government agreed to honor all Spanish land claims. Government officials continued to establish legal ownership for two decades. Finally, in 1824, the federal government established territorial courts to settle land claims. There were 126 land claims filed with the Arkansas Superior Court involving land sold by the Bowie brothers. Initially, the court upheld the land sales, but subsequent investigation revealed the Bowies had never held title to the land. The Arkansas court concluded that the original documents were forgeries and reversed its earlier decision, and the Bowies appealed. The case made its way to the U.S. Supreme

Court, which upheld the reversal. The case against the Bowie brothers was dropped when the documents in question disappeared and the plaintiffs chose not to take additional legal action.

Knife-Fighter

Despite his reputation as a land speculator, it was a knife fight in which Bowie gained a worldwide reputation. In 1826, Bowie became involved in an ongoing dispute with Norris Wright, the sheriff of Rapides Parish. The dispute began when Wright, who was also a banker, denied Bowie's loan application. Bowie then supported Wright's opponent in the election for sheriff. In Alexandria, Bowie and Wright argued in the street before Wright discharged a firearm at Bowie. The shot, which missed Bowie, infuriated him and he attacked Wright, attempting to kill him with his bare hands. Others stepped in and broke up the fight. After this experience, however, Bowie decided that he would never be without his knife again.[1] The knife boasted an enormous blade measuring 9.25 inches long and 1.5 inches wide.

A year later, in September 1827, Bowie and Wright attended a duel on a sandbar outside Natchez, Mississippi. The two men, each accompanied by several friends, supported opposing men in the duel. It ended after the duelists each fired two harmless shots and then came together to shake hands. At the conclusion of the duel, the real fight began. Talking turned to arguing, which in turn led to fighting between the two groups. The subsequent fracas, known as the Sandbar Fight, escalated when one of Wright's friends shot Bowie in the hip. Although wounded, Bowie drew a knife and rushed at the shooter. The shooter, holding an empty pistol, used the firearm as a club, striking Bowie on the head with enough force to break the weapon and knock him to the ground. Wright and Bowie then shot at each other, while Bowie remained on the ground.

The Bowie knife is a style of knife designed by Jim Bowie. The Bowie knife became popular due to its unique shape and utility as a weapon, as well as a tool for camping, fishing, and hunting. It remains popular among sportsmen even today.

At this point, Wright unsheathed his sword cane, charged at Bowie, and pierced him in the chest with his blade. The blade stuck and Wright tried to pull it out of Bowie by placing his foot on Bowie's chest, at which point Bowie pulled Wright to the ground and fatally stabbed him in the abdomen. Bowie suffered yet another stabbing and gunshot wound before the brawl ended. Fortunately for Bowie, doctors had attended the duel as a precaution and were on hand to tend to his wounds. Newspapers around the country publicized the incident, which served to popularize Bowie and the so-called Bowie knife.

Bowie Goes to Texas

After he recovered from his wounds, Bowie left Louisiana for Texas in early 1828. The Mexican Constitution of 1824 was in effect, and Texas was one of the federated states under that government. Under that constitution, Roman Catholicism was the state religion. Bowie converted to the Catholic faith, receiving his baptism on April 28, 1828, in San Antonio de Bexar. He traveled back to the United States where he was briefly engaged, but his fiancée died two weeks before they were to wed. Bowie then left Louisiana on January 1, 1830. This time, he intended to stay in Texas. Arriving in Nacogdoches, Bowie met with empresario Stephen F. Austin to apply for residency. Since Mexican citizens received preference in land grants, Bowie pledged his allegiance to Mexico and went on his way to San Antonio. Soon after he arrived there, Bowie won election as commander in the civilian militia group charged with defending settlers, later known as the Texas Rangers.

Bowie immersed himself in Mexican culture. His fluency in Spanish helped him acclimate to the environs and gain acceptance with local residents. San Antonio was a thriving city in 1830, boasting a population of about 2,500. Mexicans constituted most of Bexar's population. After promising to build some textile mills, Bowie became a Mexican citizen on September 30 of that year. He also entered into a business partnership with Juan Martín de Veramendi, the vice governor of the province. As a citizen of Mexico, Bowie could now purchase large amounts of land from the Mexican government. Ever the land speculator, Bowie persuaded several other residents to apply for land and give it to him. In a short time, Bowie owned some 700,000 acres of land, all available for reselling. Mexico City soon learned of the practice and enacted legislation in 1834 and 1835 to prohibit such speculation.

Bowie married Ursula, the 19-year-old daughter of Veramendi, his business partner, on April 25, 1831. Although he was 35 years old, Bowie listed his age as 30 in the dowry contract. Bowie also claimed an inflated net worth, most of it tied down in land. Whether he actually owned the land is arguable, given his history with land grants and titles. Bowie and his bride constructed a dwelling on land provided by Veramendi. Within two years, the couple had two children, a daughter and a son, and lived with the vice governor in the Veramendi mansion.

The Lost Mine

Bowie also gained fame in Mexico over an expedition to discover the lost Los Almagres mine. Rumored to lie near the Santa Cruz de San Sabá ruins west of San Antonio, no one knew exactly where the silver mine was located. Stories described how Apache Indians had operated the mine before Spanish officials seized it. After winning its independence from Spain, the newly established Mexican government had other problems to worry about than the silver mine. Various Indian tribes, most of them openly hostile to encroachments, threatened all mining attempts, and, since Mexico City refused to supply troops to protect mining operations, all efforts were abandoned.

After receiving the blessing of Mexican authorities, Bowie organized an expedition comprised of himself, his brother Rezin, and nine others. The party of 11 departed Bexar on November 2, 1831, and headed into hostile territory in search of the silver mine. Just six miles from the intended destination, the group encountered a large Indian force. Bowie tried to negotiate, but to no avail. The small group fought against a force perhaps 10 times its size for more than 12 hours.

Back in San Antonio, Comanche Indians arrived and reported seeing a large raiding party shadowing Bowie's expedition. San Antonio residents, including Bowie's wife, Ursula, presumed Bowie's party dead. Instead, Bowie and his men valiantly fought off their attackers, killing as many as 40 Indians while losing only one man. They returned to Bexar a few days later, to the amazement of all. Bowie discovered his wife in mourning, a mourning that quickly turned to joy. Bowie's report of the expedition's events, written in Spanish, was soon published throughout Mexico. These exploits enhanced his reputation as a fighter. Bowie searched once more for the mine, but a two-and-a-half-month search revealed no clues as to the location of the lost silver mine of Los Almagres.

Rising Tensions

Beginning in 1830, the Mexican Congress adopted several legislative acts restricting Anglo rights in the Mexican province of Texas, especially property rights. Understandably, transplanted Americans residing in Texas did not care for the changes to the legal code and offered their objections to Mexican authorities, both locally and in Mexico City. The Mexican government responded by increasing its military presence throughout the province. San Antonio de Bexar received its complement of troops. The military was loyal to President Anastasio Bustamante, who seemed to dislike the presence of so many Americans. Discontent rose, and in 1832, Anglos supported Antonio de Santa Anna when he led a revolt against Bustamante. In Nacogdoches, troops still loyal to the sitting president demanded the disarming of all residents.

Bowie joined others in marching to Nacogdoches to protest the pronouncement in early August 1832. Arriving in town, the group had not yet reached the municipal building to deliver their concerns and demands when a Mexican unit of 100 cavalry attacked them. Defending themselves, the Texians fired on the troops, the cavalry retreated, and the Texians laid siege to the fort. The Mexicans endured another assault, losing 33 soldiers. During the night, the Mexicans abandoned the city and took flight. The Texians harassed them for a time, but allowed the fleeing force to escape.

The Texians decided to work through political channels and called for a meeting to deliberate and propose constructive changes to the Mexican government. James Bowie attended the resulting meeting, the Convention of 1833, as a delegate. The convention asked the Mexican government to recognize Texas as a separate state within the Mexican federation.

A cholera outbreak struck Texas in late summer. In his concern that the epidemic would spread to San Antonio, Bowie sent his daughter and pregnant wife with her parents to the family home in Monclova. Ursula and her whole family contracted cholera and succumbed to the disease, dying before mid-September. Word reached Bowie in November while he was conducting business in Natchez. The knife-fighter drowned his grief in liquor. For the rest of his days, Bowie lost himself in alcohol and became "careless in his dress."[2]

Politically, the tension between Mexico and the Texians abated as Mexico altered the laws regulating land sales. Bowie could again make a living off land speculation. The Mexican government even appointed Bowie one of its land commissioners, a post he held until President Antonio Lopez de Santa Anna did away with the Coahuila y Tejas government. At the same time, Santa Anna directed Mexican officials to arrest any Texians conducting business in Monclova. Once Bowie realized that his position offered no protection, he returned to the Austin settlements in the east.

President Santa Anna now turned on the Texians by abolishing the provincial government and increasing the reach of the federal government located in Mexico City. Many of the Anglos in Texas no longer trusted the Mexican government and began to advocate taking up arms to ensure Texian rights. The so-called War Party enjoyed support from many within Texas. As the War Party increased in popularity, Santa Anna viewed

Texians as a threat. The new leader decided to send more troops to Texas to discourage military action. Santa Anna's actions led Bowie to support the War Party.

WILLIAM B. TRAVIS

William Barret Travis was born in Saluda County, South Carolina, in August 1809. At age nine, he moved with his parents to Sparta, Alabama. He attended school in Claiborne and later worked there as an assistant teacher. After teaching for a time, Travis began practicing law as an apprentice to an attorney in Claiborne. At 19, he married a former student, Rosanna Cato, in October 1828. Rosanna was just 16 years old when they wed. She became pregnant soon after and gave birth to a son in August the following year. The young attorney joined the Masonic Temple, published a paper, and served in the local Alabama state militia.

Pressure mounted on the young husband and father as William and Rosanna expected another child. Perhaps the couple experienced conflict within the marriage. For whatever reason, in early 1831, Travis fled west to Texas, leaving behind his pregnant wife and young son. Rosanna filed for divorce, which was granted on January 9, 1836.

Travis in Texas

When Travis reached Texas in 1831, he did so illegally. Seeking to stem the tide of Americans entering Texas, Mexico had enacted legislation forbidding additional immigration to Texas. Travis traveled to San Felipe and purchased land from Stephen F. Austin. Though he was still married, he recorded his marital status as single. He established a law practice in Anahuac, a port situated on the eastern end of Galveston Bay. While familiarizing himself with Spanish, Travis practiced law and joined the War Party, the group of militants opposed to centralized Mexican rule in Texas. His involvement with the War Party eventually led to a confrontation that helped spark increased demands for Texas rights and statehood. Travis's radical activities led to his arrest in 1832, whereupon a Texian mob intimidated Mexican officials who released him. True to his character, Travis persisted in his criticism of the Mexican government.

Following the disturbances at Anahuac, Travis relocated to San Felipe where he won acceptance by the civic leaders. He met and began courting Rebecca Cummings, whom he intended to marry when his divorce was finalized.

Following the Convention of 1833, later that April, Stephen Austin personally appealed to government authorities in Mexico City, relaying the concerns of the Anglo settlers. When officials promised to repeal the law forbidding immigration, Austin started back for Texas, but Santa Anna ordered him arrested and put him in jail in January 1834 where he languished until August 1835. While Austin remained in prison, leaders in East Texas remained calm so as not to endanger him, but once he was released, tensions again rose. At about the same time, Santa Anna claimed still more powers for the central government of Mexico. Finally, even mild-mannered Stephen Austin was calling for war and independence. The War Party agenda was now the preferred course of action.

Santa Anna restored the military garrison and customhouse in Anahuac to reassert Mexican authority. Travis received authorization from those favoring war to drive the force from Anahuac. Travis led about two dozen men on an amphibious assault from Galveston Bay in which they successfully captured the Mexican garrison in late June 1835. Although hailed by some, those favoring peace with Mexico believed that Travis's actions created more problems for the settlers. Many labeled him a rabble-rouser. General Martín Perfecto de Cos, who commanded the northern Mexican forces, went to San Antonio, where he demanded that the other colonists turn them over to face a military tribunal.

Travis was one of the many Texians who joined the militia and rushed to defy General Cos at Gonzales in October, but he

Pictured is a drawing of Lieutenant Colonel William Barret Travis, commander of the Texian army, during the battle for independence from Mexico. His famous "Victory or Death" letter helped to motivate the Texian army and rallied support for the cause of Texan independence.

arrived after the battle ended. He stayed on as a scout, taking part in the siege of Bexar. Before the Texians waged the final battle that drove Cos from San Antonio, Travis returned to San Felipe where he received a commission as a lieutenant colonel in the cavalry from American-born governor of Mexican-governed Texas Henry Smith. His post required him to recruit a force of 100 men and report to San Antonio in support of Colonel James Neill. He managed to attract just 29 riders to join him. Ashamed, Travis asked the governor to be relieved of command. Smith refused, and Travis did his duty—he went to San Antonio in January 1836.

William Barret Travis was a brash young man who exuded confidence in himself. Many perceived his poise as arrogance. One of Travis's close friends and former employees, J.H. Kuykendall, described the young adventurer as "able and honest" but also said he had a "brusque manner" and could be "loud and somewhat harsh" with others.[3] As one historian put it, Travis "had an abrasive personality."[4] It is clear the man was talented and possessed many gifts for leadership, but few people actually liked him.

When James Neill, the commanding officer at the Alamo, received permission to leave his post on February 13 to care for his ailing family, he named Lieutenant Colonel William Travis as commander in his stead, although James Bowie was both older and more experienced than Travis. Still, Neill and Travis both held commissions in the Texian army, while Bowie was a colonel in the volunteer militia. Neill's decision was consistent with military protocol, which favored the regulars over the militia. At just 26 years old, Travis found himself commanding officer of a small outpost in Texas: the Alamo.

DAVID (DAVY) CROCKETT

Davy Crockett was born on August 17, 1786, in rural Tennessee. Scholars are unsure exactly where, but they do know he was the fifth of nine children born to John and Rebecca Hawkins

From humble beginnings in a log cabin in Tennessee to pioneer, congressman, and patriot, Davy Crockett's story is one of legend. The most common account of Crockett's fate was that he was killed in the final minutes of the Battle of the Alamo. Some accounts claim that he survived the siege and was later executed by General Santa Anna.

Crockett. His father was a veteran of the Revolutionary War. Crockett's grandfather was the first in the family to move west, building a home in present-day Tennessee. Thus, Davy grew up on the frontier, exposed to the many dangers and struggles of living in Indian country.

As a young boy, Crockett went to school, but he dropped out at age 13 over an incident in which he successfully stood up to a school bully, beating him in a schoolyard fight. When his teacher intended to punish Davy with the standard paddling, the youngster wanted none of it. He left home each day for school, but did not attend. The teacher sent a letter to Crockett's father seeking an explanation for Davy's truancy. When his father confronted him, Davy, resisting what he believed to be an unfair punishment, "took to his heels" and left home.[5] Crockett spent the next few years roaming through the Tennessee countryside, herding cattle sometimes and living off

SAM HOUSTON
(1793–1863)

Not a Hero of the Alamo

Although he was not present at the siege and battle of the Alamo, Sam Houston is often the center of debate concerning it. While his critics claim that Houston should have reinforced the Alamo, defenders point out that the commander ordered the destruction and abandonment of the mission. Aware of the controversy, Houston wrote about the quandary of being compared to martyrs, calling the Alamo leaders "brave and gallant spirits."* In response to his critics, Houston conjured up the image of Travis, Crockett, and Bowie, claiming that "these brave and manly heroes," if they could speak from the grave, "would look down upon my insignificant and wicked slanderers with withering scorn and contempt."** Houston reasoned that, since he and those who fell at the Alamo all fought for independence, the criticism and blame over mistakes in judgment were inappropriate.

After the revolution, Houston twice held the office of president of the Republic of Texas, and he also served as a U.S. senator after the land, honing his skills as a hunter and trapper. At age 16, Crockett stopped for a meal at an inn belonging to his father. One of his sisters recognized him, "sprang up and seized him about the neck, and proclaimed his return."[6] All was forgiven as the family welcomed him back home.

Young Crockett became engaged in October 1805 to Margaret Elder. The couple filed the contract of marriage, but the wedding never occurred. Evidently, Margaret changed her mind, broke off the engagement, and married another man. Crockett seemingly recovered from the emotional blow and married Mary (Polly) Finley less than a year later, in August 1806. The

Texas joined the Union in 1845. During the Mexican-American War (1846–1848), President James Polk extended the rank of general to Houston, but the hero of San Jacinto rejected the offer. Later, in 1859, Houston won election as governor of Texas. When South Carolina and other Southern states seceded, Houston argued against secession and refused to take an oath of allegiance to the Confederacy. Texas turned on its hero, removed him from office, and joined the Confederacy anyway. His own children deserted him over the issue. Houston returned home, though many viewed him a traitor. As the great conflict raged, Houston lay in his bed, dying on July 26, 1863. His last words, spoken to his wife, were "Texas, Margaret, Texas."*** The city of Houston, Texas, bears his name as a lasting tribute to this early leader of Texas independence.

---

* *John B. Shackford, ed.* David Crockett: The Man and the Legend. *Chapel Hill: The University of North Carolina Press, 1956, 226.*
***Ibid.*
***Hoyt, The Alamo, *147.*

union produced two sons and a daughter. Polly died and Crockett remarried in 1816, fathering another three children.

In September 1813, Crockett joined the Tennessee militia to fight in the Creek War. Conflicts with the Indians and later their British allies kept Crockett in the militia throughout the War of 1812 (a war between the United States and Great Britain that lasted until spring of 1815). Crockett was among those who marched south and fought in the Battle of Horseshoe Bend under Andrew Jackson. On March 27, 1815, Crockett received his discharge papers from the militia. Three years later, his regiment voted him the rank of lieutenant colonel.

Politician

In 1821, Crockett decided to try his hand at politics. He won election to the Committee of Propositions and Grievances in 1821. He successfully ran for a seat in the U.S. House of Representatives in 1826 and 1828. As a member of Congress, Crockett favored squatters' rights. Squatters were individuals who moved onto western lands before the government surveyed and sold the property. Government law at the time prohibited squatters who held no titles to land from purchasing it. Crockett, a backwoodsman from the frontier, fought against this policy. The Tennessee congressman also opposed President Andrew Jackson's Indian policy. The president still had many powerful friends in Tennessee and used his influence to defeat Crockett in the 1830 election. Crockett recovered and regained his seat in 1832 but then lost a close race filled with questionable voting practices in the fall of 1835. Stung by yet another political defeat, Crockett left politics and Tennessee behind. Since the voters had rejected him, Crockett told the voters, "You may all go to hell and I will go to Texas."[7]

As he wrote, "I want to explore the Texas well before I return."[8] On October 31, 1835, Crockett finalized plans to travel to Texas and on November 1 the Tennessee frontiersman began his journey. He reached Nacogdoches, Texas, after the

first of the year. His initial impression of Texas was very posi-
tive; he said it was "the garden spot of the world" and held "the
best land and the best prospects for health."[9] More important,
he believed that the land itself was "a fortune to any man to
come here. There is a world here to settle."[10] Texas had captured the Tennessee frontiersman's imagination and allegiance.
Within days, he had signed an oath to support the Provisional
Government of Texas and volunteered to serve in the fight for
independence. In return for his six-month military commitment, the Provisional Government promised Crockett and
each recruit nearly 4,600 acres of land. Before heading west,
Crockett sent one last letter home to his family. "Do not be
uneasy about me," he wrote, "I am with my friends."[11] Following orders, Crockett and a few others traveled to San Antonio
de Bexar. Exactly one month before the fall of the Alamo, on
February 6, Crockett rode into San Antonio for the first time.
It was there that he met Bowie and Travis.

The Alamo

Prior to the surrender agreement at San Antonio de Bexar on December 10, 1835, while General Cos was doing his best to keep Mexico's hold on the town, Santa Anna traveled to San Luis Potosi. Arriving there on December 5, the "Napoleon of the West" prepared to smash the rebellion. San Antonio lay some 700 miles north of San Luis Potosi. Lacking government funds, Santa Anna spent his own money to raise and equip an army. Still short, he borrowed what he needed and outfitted a force of at least 6,000 men. Then, by the end of December, he led his army north.

Meanwhile, in Texas, rebel leaders faced the prospect of defending the vast southern front against Mexico. Not knowing exactly where the Mexicans might strike, Houston and his officers decided to secure the beach at Copano, the fort at Goliad, and the Alamo mission. The Texians believed each of these three locations crucial to their defense. Texian leaders were also convinced that no Mexican army could reach them before spring, probably in mid-April. Such an assumption was a reasonable one. Santa Anna's army was forced to endure cold nights, frigid winds, and blinding blizzards as it traversed the desert land separating it from the Alamo. Only the determination of its leader kept the army moving toward San Antonio. Santa Anna viewed the Alamo as key to reasserting control over Texas, writing in 1837, "Bexar was held by the enemy and it was necessary to open the door to our future operations by taking it."[1]

On December 7, 1835, General Santa Anna issued orders to his troops concerning the future fighting with the Texas insurgents. Santa Anna characterized the Texians as enemies of the state, stating, "They have, with audacity, declared a war of extermination to the Mexicans and they should be treated in the same way."[2] Thus, Santa Anna hinted at future actions in which the Mexicans would take no prisoners and offer neither paroles nor mercy to rebellious settlers. The Mexican general did not know it at the time, but the Texians were not engaged in a war of extermination—indeed, the rebels paroled General Cos and his men on December 11, just four days after Santa Anna asserted his vision for the kind of war he intended to wage. Nevertheless, Santa Anna's orders declared, "The foreigners who are making war against the Mexican nation, violating all laws, are not deserving of any consideration, and for that reason, no quarter will be given them."[3] The president of Mexico intended to put down the revolt decisively.

SAN ANTONIO DE BEXAR AND THE ALAMO

The Alamo was the site of the first mission founded in San Antonio, Texas. The first Spanish people to enter Texas came in the 1530s, survivors of the failed Narváez expedition to Florida's west coast in 1527. After failing to establish a colony in Florida, these Spaniards constructed crude boats and sailed for Cuba. Storms sank many of the vessels, but one eventually "landed on a small island off the coast of Texas, near present-day Galveston."[4] Four of the men from this boat eventually walked several hundred miles, arriving in Mexico City in 1536. Their tales of golden cities led to the famed Coronado expedition (of 1540–1542, through New Mexico, Texas, Oklahoma, and Kansas). For much of the next two centuries, Spain seemed more interested in finding possible treasure in Texas than in establishing settlements there. The Spanish approach shifted in 1718, when missionaries led by Father Antonio Olivares began building a mission he called San Antonio de Valero, both as a tribute to Marquis de Valero, the viceroy of Mexico, and in honor of St. Anthony of Padua. The priest situated the mission on the San Antonio River on May 15. Four days later, Spanish authorities founded a military garrison they called Presidio San Antonio de Bexar. Officials also laid out the plans for a town, La Villa de Bexar. Due to its location on the frontier, however, the village never developed. At the time of the 1836 battle, many referred to the area as Bexar. Today, San Antonio lies within Bexar County.

The Alamo was one of a series of missions founded along the San Antonio River. The establishment of a military fort so near the mission led to the development of two different plazas. One of the Texians who helped capture Bexar in November and December 1835, artillery commander Captain William R. Carey, described the separation of the military and the church and the layout of the community:

> This place is an ancient Mexican fort & Town divided by a small river which eminates from Springs. The town has two Squares in and the church in the centre, one a military and the other a government square. The Alamo or the fort as we call it, is a very old building, built for the purpose of protecting the citizens from hostile Indians.[5]

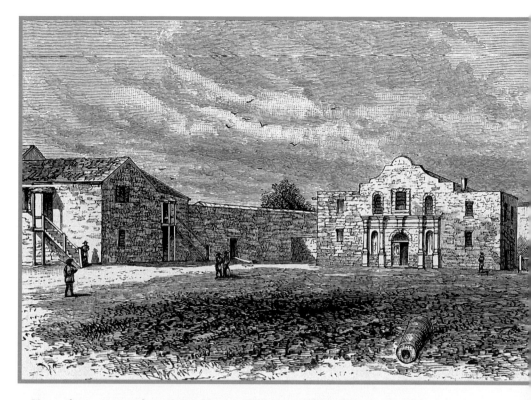

Above is an engraving of the Alamo. This former Franciscan mission was built in 1722 by the Spanish for the education of local American Indians after their conversion to Christianity. The compound later became a fortress and was nearly in ruins after the Battle of the Alamo in 1836.

The two squares provided both the Mexican and Texian forces a plaza from which to conduct their operations: Santa Anna within the village, Travis within the Alamo.

In 1724, church authorities moved the mission for the third time, to its present site, laying the cornerstone for the current chapel on May 8, 1744. Missionary efforts declined after 1765, leading to the abandonment of the Alamo in 1793 when church records were relocated to the San Fernando Cathedral. Ten years later, a group of Spanish soldiers from the town of Alamo de Parras took up residence in the mission while garrisoned in

San Antonio. Historians are unsure of how and why the mission became known as the Alamo. Perhaps the first Spanish soldiers to reside there referred to it as the Alamo, a shortened version of their home. Others believe the name originated from the nearby clusters of cottonwood trees, or *los alamos*, lining the irrigation ditches.[6]

Due to its location, Spanish government officials used Bexar as the capital from which they administered Texas. Typically, the Spanish military commander stationed in Bexar also served as the governor. When Mexico won its independence in 1821 and adopted its Constitution of 1824, government affairs over Texas were administered from Coahuila, and Bexar no longer served as the seat of power for Texas. Coahuila did use Bexar as the location for the government of the Department of Bexar. The Coahuila governor even named Bexar the state capital of Coahuila y Tejas in May 1835, but the Texas Revolution prevented the relocation of the state government.

Originally, the Catholic Church had built the Alamo for use as a church. Thus, the Alamo fort was more a compilation of various attempts to make the church more defensible than it was a defensive military stronghold. The compound itself was a series of walls, erected during the eighteenth century, that connected the buildings and huts to prevent Indian raiders from openly riding into the church plaza. One historian describes the Alamo as "a fortified village whose structures were laid out around the perimeter of a three-acre rectangle."[7] A plaza was situated inside the perimeter, while the church sat on the southeast corner of the compound.

Although the military had made defensive modifications to the Alamo over time, the complex was designed not for military purposes but for religious ones. The church had walls more than 20 feet high and as thick as 4 feet, but it lacked a roof. Unfortunately, the church was the most defensively sound portion of the fort. The rest of the walls "were only about a foot thick and less than half the height of the church."[8] The garrison had two weak points: the north wall and the palisade. When Texians forced Cos and his force to surrender in December 1835, Texian artillery pounded the north wall, creating a gap there. The Mexicans repaired the gap, but just before they vacated the fort, they undid their repairs, leaving a gap for the returning Texians to deal with. The final Mexican assault on the Alamo on March 6 concentrated on the north wall. The other weak point, the palisade, was a makeshift wall constructed to link the church and the low barracks. Consisting of two rows of vertical logs with dirt packed between them, the palisade sealed the space most open on the perimeter. The proficiency of Crockett and his sharpshooters, who served at the palisade during the siege, helped reduce most of the structural weaknesses of this portion of the fortifications.

An 1831 census numbered Bexar's population at 1,634.[9] Most estimates increase that figure to about 2,000 in 1836.[10] In late 1835, the Mexicans buttressed their defenses by erecting earthen cannon ramps and platforms at key points along the wall. After driving the Mexicans out, the Texian volunteers constructed the palisade to shore up the defensibility of the fort. In front of the palisade, the defenders placed sharpened stakes facing outward to deter enemy cavalry and soldiers from attacking there. The Texians also continued to repair the north wall during the siege to improve their chances of holding out. Even with artillery pieces and the addition of a stockade wall, however, the Alamo lacked many of the basic needs of a militarily defensible stronghold.

DISCORD AND PREPARATION

As Santa Anna made his way north to San Antonio, the Alamo defenders seemed to be in no hurry to make preparations for an assault, as they did not expect the Mexican force to arrive until the middle of March. To add to the difficulties, the absence of Colonel Neill led to a rift between the two ranking officers. William Travis commanded about 30 regulars while Jim Bowie led about 120 volunteers of the militia. When Neill left, he put Travis in command, but many of the militia resisted the rigid schedule and army discipline Travis expected of them. Worse still, Travis and Bowie feuded. Travis believed Bowie to be a drunkard and unprofessional, while the knife-fighter found his younger counterpart arrogant and uncompromising. Facing unrest, Travis used a militia solution to leadership problems: He called for an election. The vote split the men, with the militia choosing Bowie and the regulars favoring Travis, as might be expected. The Alamo now had two commanders, who reached an arrangement whereby "Travis would command the cavalry, both regular and volunteer, while Bowie commanded the fortress itself, and Neill, when he returned, would be superior to both."[11] The arrangement was far from ideal. The two commanders agreed to cosign all official correspondence. In truth, Travis had little choice. Without Bowie and the troublesome volunteers, there could be no defense of the Alamo.

Further complicating the defense efforts were the lingering effects of the Matamoros expedition (the controversial expedition to attack Matamoros, Tamaulipas, during the Texas Revolution), which had depleted the Alamo of the supplies, men, tools, and virtually anything else necessary to shore up the defenses. The arrival on February 8 of Davy Crockett, who led a group of 14 men into the Alamo, boosted morale. Unfortunately, the small outpost needed far more men and supplies than the Tennessee Mounted Rifles. Word reached the defenders that Santa Anna and a large Mexican force had crossed the Rio Grande and was heading toward San Antonio.

SANTA ANNA ARRIVES

When daylight dawned on Tuesday, February 23, 1836, the town of San Antonio was suddenly bustling with activity. The native inhabitants of the village—men, women, and children—were leaving their homes, taking oxcarts, wagons, mules, and horses laden with their personal belongings, jostling each other in the crowded streets. Colonel Travis sensed that something was wrong. He questioned several locals who insisted that everyone was leaving as part of annual preparations for the spring planting season. Yet Travis suspected that something more ominous had led to this seemingly spontaneous evacuation.

Hoping to stem the flow, Travis sent out orders commanding the locals to remain in San Antonio, but the tumult just intensified as more and more townspeople left in spite of them. Travis arrested several villagers to question them and even resorted to threats, but it was no use: The local townspeople continued to leave under the pretense of preparing to plant their crops.

By late morning, Travis was annoyed at the situation. Around 11:00 A.M., a pleasant native appeared before Travis, claiming to have important information for him. Travis listened attentively as the Tejano explained why everyone was leaving. A messenger had arrived late the night before, bringing word that General Santa Anna, who was near San Antonio, wanted all loyal residents to leave at daybreak. Although the story explained the odd behavior of local villagers, it seemed incredible to Travis that Santa Anna could already be so close to San Antonio.

Neither Travis nor Bowie felt prepared to face the Mexican troops. In the previous weeks, the two commanders had spent most of their time and energy trying to gain sole command and failed to organize a method for scouting the surrounding countryside. Thus, Travis had no idea whether or not to believe the report of a large Mexican force approaching his position. Travis and Dr. John Sutherland climbed to the top of the highest point in town, the San Fernando Church belfry. From that vantage point, the two looked in vain for signs of an approaching army. Travis then ordered Private Daniel W. Cloud to stay in the belfry and remain on the lookout. Around 1:00 P.M., Cloud began ringing the bell. Several defenders, including Travis, ascended the belfry, but the enemy was not in sight. The volunteers were still unsure whether Santa Anna's army was nearby.

Travis directed two scouts to survey the surrounding area. Dr. John Sutherland and John W. Smith, the future mayor of San Antonio, headed west out of town, on horseback. After traveling about a mile and a half, the two reached the top of a small rise and found themselves within 150 yards of several hundred cavalry troops. Smith and Sutherland quickly retraced their route. Before leaving town, the two had explained to Travis that, when they returned, any pace other than a walk would communicate the presence of a Mexican force. The two men spurred their horses into a full gallop. Recent rains had left the road muddy. Sutherland's horse stumbled and fell, landing on the doctor's legs. The horse lay stunned for a few moments, keeping the doctor pinned down. Finally, the horse arose and the two scouts resumed their mad dash to San Antonio. The San Fernando Church bell rang continuously as the belfry sentry saw the signal and sounded the alarm. Travis had decided that the mission grounds provided the best defensive position. He then ordered his men to abandon the town and pull back within the Alamo compound.

Crockett met the two scouts when they reentered San Antonio. Dr. Sutherland nursed an injured knee. The frontiersman helped the doctor across the San Antonio River while Smith hurried to his house in order to gather his belongings. After reaching the Alamo, Sutherland made his report to Travis. There was no longer any doubt: The Mexican troops had arrived.

Travis acted quickly to supply the fort and send for reinforcements. His men scoured the village, searching through homes, businesses, warehouses, and barns, taking anything of use that they could find. The searchers found grain, equipment, and 30 head of cattle, all of which they took with them into the Alamo. Some of the defenders, however, had other concerns

The most popular means of transferring information was by
courier on horseback. These missions were dangerous as,
even at breakneck speed, sometimes a courier could not reach
his destination in time or failed to make it because he was
captured, wounded, or killed. On February 23, 1836, William
Travis dispatched two couriers with pleas for reinforcements.
A total of 32 reinforcements reached the Alamo.

than the security of the fort. James Bowie visited the home of his late wife's family, taking two adopted sisters and an infant boy into the Alamo. Captain Almeron Dickinson gathered up his wife, Susannah; their 15-month-old daughter, Angelina; and all their belongings from their home in San Antonio.

As his men searched for necessary supplies, Travis quickly wrote two letters seeking reinforcements. One he dispatched to Goliad, located 95 miles from the Alamo, where James W. Fannin commanded 400 to 450 men. Travis begged Fannin to send some of these troops. Travis also gave a letter to Dr. Sutherland, addressed "To any of the inhabitants of Texas." He quickly got to the point: "The enemy in large force is in sight—We want men & provisions—Send them to us—We have 150 men & are determined to defend the Alamo to the last—Give us assistance."[12]

Travis gave the communiqué to Dr. Sutherland who left on horseback with John Smith, another courier seeking reinforcements from Gonzales. Nat Lewis, a shopkeeper from San Antonio accompanied them on foot. It was now midafternoon, around 3:00 P.M., and as they left town, the three men turned and observed the first units of the Mexican cavalry entering the military plaza. The Mexicans were now in San Antonio. Smith and Sutherland decided to separate from Lewis and cut across the country to avoid detection and capture by Mexican patrols.

Shortly after his advance units secured the plaza, General Santa Anna arrived. A military band marked his arrival. His staff, standard-bearers, and several hundred foot soldiers also escorted the general into the city. Additional troops continued to trickle in throughout the coming hours and days. After surveying the scene and hearing the report of the volunteers in the Alamo, Santa Anna ordered a large red flag hung from the belfry of the San Fernando Church. Mexicans used the red flag to communicate that they would show no mercy to their foes. The general wanted the rebels to know there would be no quarter—they would take no prisoners, give no paroles, offer no mercy—to any of the volunteers within the fort.

THE SIEGE BEGINS

Within the Alamo, William Travis saw the banner and decided to respond in his own way. Although he shared command with Bowie, Travis independently ordered the firing of his largest gun, the 18-pound cannon, toward the town and the Mexican force. The shot did neither harm nor damage, but Travis's brazen act signified Texian intentions to resist. Santa Anna retorted by firing four shots that also landed harmlessly within the walls of the Alamo. James Butler Bonham, who was just then returning from Goliad, rushed to the Alamo. He brought word that Colonel Fannin had concluded that his orders required him to keep all 400-plus of his men to hold Goliad.

Meanwhile, the split command began to tear apart. James Bowie was angry with Travis for firing a shot toward town. Such a display served no point other than to endanger negotiations and waste a cannonball. Bowie sent a messenger, the adventurer Green B. Jameson, to the Mexicans to seek an "honorable truce" with Santa Anna.[13] Although he did not use the garrison's 18-pound cannon to show his defiance, Bowie ended his written message by crossing out the customary "God and the Mexican Federation" and replaced it with "God and Texas."[14]

The intentional insult was not lost on Santa Anna. The Mexican general coolly ordered his underling to respond in an equally curt manner. Santa Anna rejected discussing terms "with rebellious foreigners to whom there is no other recourse left, if they wish to save their lives, than to place themselves immediately at the disposal of the Supreme Government."[15] Travis understood Santa Anna's terms as unconditional surrender, something he was unwilling to accept.

Travis then sent his own messenger, Albert Martin, to the Mexican lines to discuss terms with Santa Anna's secretary, Colonel Juan N. Almonte. Fluent in English, Almonte reiterated Santa Anna's demands that the defenders lay down their arms and surrender.

Santa Anna and his staff set up their headquarters in town, in a house located on the main square. The general grew angry that more of his troops were not already in Bexar—in fact, portions of his army stretched back for miles. Also lagging behind were additional artillery pieces that the general badly needed

VICTORY OR DEATH

While trapped inside the Alamo, Colonel William B. Travis penned some inspirational letters in which he asked for help against the Mexican force led by Santa Anna. Following the Texas Revolution, many of these letters were published, and they shamed the Texians for not doing more to help their comrades inside the mission compound. One message is particularly striking due to the clarity in which Travis describes their plight and states his intention to fight to the end. Sent out on the second day of the siege, this message "has been considered one of the most heroic in American history."* It stated the following:

Fellow Citizens & Compatriots—I am besieged by a thousand or more of the Mexicans under Santa Anna. I have sustained a continual bombardment and cannonade for 24 hours & have not lost a man. The enemy has demanded a surrender at discretion, otherwise the garrison are to be put to the sword, if the fort is taken. I have answered the demand with a cannon shot, & our for a prolonged siege. The impatient leader and his general staff began devising their strategy for taking the Alamo.

Throughout the night, the Mexicans fired their cannon at the Alamo. Inside the walls, the volunteers strengthened their positions and hoped for reinforcements. All the while, random cannon fire kept the men on edge. The only harm to the defenders came in the afternoon, when an artillery blast injured a single horse.

The Mexicans lost at least one man the first day. Renowned sharpshooter Davy Crockett felled a soldier who unwisely

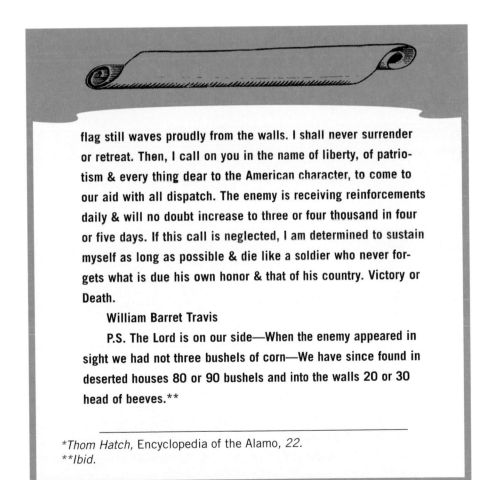

flag still waves proudly from the walls. I shall never surrender or retreat. Then, I call on you in the name of liberty, of patriotism & every thing dear to the American character, to come to our aid with all dispatch. The enemy is receiving reinforcements daily & will no doubt increase to three or four thousand in four or five days. If this call is neglected, I am determined to sustain myself as long as possible & die like a soldier who never forgets what is due his own honor & that of his country. Victory or Death.

William Barret Travis

P.S. The Lord is on our side—When the enemy appeared in sight we had not three bushels of corn—We have since found in deserted houses 80 or 90 bushels and into the walls 20 or 30 head of beeves.**

*Thom Hatch, Encyclopedia of the Alamo, *22.*
**Ibid.

approached the river near the west wall of the compound. At his request, Crockett and his men were assigned to defend the south stockade wall that ran between the long barracks and the chapel. This was undoubtedly the most vulnerable portion of the Alamo defenses. It would later serve as the stage for some of the most brutal fighting of the battle.

The Siege

When Santa Anna first arrived in San Antonio, accompanying him were about 1,600 of his troops. The rest were still making their way northward. The advance force had some artillery, but considering the Alamo's weaponry, the Mexican cannon were comparatively light. Santa Anna had just eight cannon: two seven-inch howitzers, two eight-pounders, two six-pounders, and two four-pounders. After securing the town on the first day, El Presidente Santa Anna implemented steps to lay siege to the Alamo.

To be successful, a siege requires the encirclement of the fort to prevent both those within from leaving and outside help from bringing in supplies and reinforcements. The besiegers then seek to draw the encirclement ever closer to allow their artillery to weaken the defenses. The goal is either to force surrender or weaken the fort to ensure a successful assault. From

Pictured is the map of the Alamo area based on General Santa Anna's original battlefield map. The Texian army was unaware that Santa Anna had begun preparations the year before and was unprepared for the arrival of the Mexican army.

February 24 until the final assault on March 6, the men inside the Alamo watched as Santa Anna continued to employ the standard approach of encircling the mission compound and squeezing his artillery ever closer to it. Without reinforcements, the eventual outcome was never in doubt. What few recognized at the outset of the siege was that the bravery of the defenders would continue to the end under these dire circumstances, nor did most realize the stunning impact on the fledgling republic of the way in which the Alamo fell.

THE SECOND DAY

Day two of the siege brought some relief to the defenders inside the fort—specifically, the resolution of the issue and difficulties of sharing command. Bowie, who commanded the volunteers, became too ill to carry out his duties. The knife-fighter relinquished his power of command to Travis. Many historians believe that Bowie suffered from typhoid fever. Other possible culprits have also been suggested, including pneumonia, his excessive drinking, and tuberculosis. Regardless of the cause, the effect was the same: Bowie spent the remainder of the siege in a small room in the lower barracks. Caring for Bowie was a Mexican sage known as Senora Candelaria. Bowie, who had married a Mexican and adopted his wife's traditions, appeared content to let Senora Candelaria provide for his medical care. Bowie was concerned that his sisters-in-law were now inside the Alamo and he himself was unable to protect them. He reassured Juana Alsbury, "Sister, do not be afraid. I leave you with Col. Travis, Col. Crockett, and other friends. They are gentlemen, and will treat you kindly."[1]

At daylight, the Texians observed a detachment of Mexicans constructing earthworks across the San Antonio River between 350 and 400 yards from the Alamo. Within hours, those surrounding the compound had placed two nine-pound cannons within the entrenchment. Each cannon was capable of firing two rounds per minute up to a distance of 1,400 yards. At twilight, the Mexicans opened fire with the two cannon and a howitzer. The blasts hit two of the Alamo's cannon, including the 18-pounder. The damage was slight, however, and the volunteers returned fire from their largest gun. The barrage ended as it got dark. Travis took advantage of the lull and the cover of darkness to send out a plea for help. Twenty-eight-year-old Albert Martin, who had injured his foot, left the compound and slipped through the Mexican lines, taking with him Travis's plea.

That night, the Mexicans attempted to make war on the Alamo using another kind of weapon: music. Military bands played loudly with horns trumpeting as a general ruckus emanated from the Mexican camp. A few defenders briefly left the fort to gather firewood while some of the locals sauntered over to the Alamo and spoke with those within. Colonel Juan

Bringas led a small Mexican scouting party to a footbridge, intending to cross it and approach the fort. When one of his men was shot dead by an Alamo defender, the alarmed Bringas fell off his horse as he wheeled about to escape. He and the remaining men of the party were unhurt. Santa Anna responded by firing artillery into the compound intermittently throughout the night, but the besiegers made no more attempts to approach the walls. The second night passed without further incidents.

DAY THREE

The third day dawned and Santa Anna decided to put the Alamo defenses to the test. The Mexicans directed a heavy artillery barrage on the main gate. Meanwhile, 300 soldiers gathered near the river and prepared to attack. The defenders recognized the artillery attack as nothing more than a diversion and prepared for the coming ground assault. Around 10:00 A.M., the assault came. The troops forded the river and approached the south wall of the fort, finding cover in small buildings lying between them and the Alamo. When that cover thinned out, about 100 yards from the walls, the Mexican troops charged.

Those within the Alamo waited patiently until the attackers were virtually on top of them, at which point the defenders fired grapeshot from the cannon and let loose a torrent of fire from rifles and other firearms. The Mexicans suffered two dead and six wounded. The assault fell back to the protection of the huts and sheds. The first attempt to storm the compound had failed.

Travis, though, recognized the danger those small buildings lying outside the Alamo presented. Davy Crockett and several other sharpshooters fired to protect a small group of volunteers who rushed out of the south gate and set the buildings on fire. The Mexicans tried again to advance and shoot at those who were setting the fires, but were pinned down by

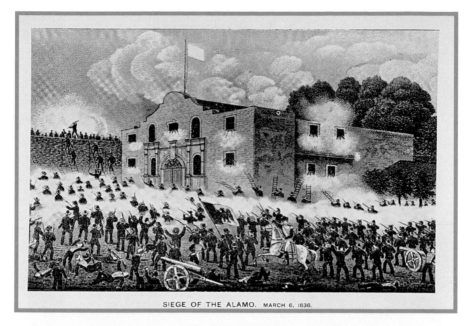

SIEGE OF THE ALAMO. MARCH 6, 1836.

Six thousand Mexican soldiers fought between 180 and 250 men from the Texian army for 13 days. The Mexican soldiers divided into four columns and rushed toward the Alamo, shouting, "Viva Santa Anna! Viva la Republica!" Any Texian soldiers that were unable to reach the barracks were killed outside the walls by the Mexican cavalry.

the defenders' rifle shots and an occasional cannon shot. The Mexican troops watched helplessly as many of the small buildings burned to the ground. Mexican artillery continued to barrage the fort while small groups of defenders ventured out to set fields and other close buildings afire. Soon, the Mexican troops began to retreat as there was too little cover to sustain their position. By noon, the attacking force had withdrawn completely.

The clash boosted the spirits of the defenders. The Texians had held their own, beaten back a direct attack from a superior force, and suffered no major injuries or deaths. Although Colonel Travis realized the seriousness of their situation, the men were excited by the day's events. The Alamo commander made his way throughout the fort, encouraging his men and doing his best to bolster their spirits even as he fully understood their perilous situation. It was true that the defenders had driven back the attackers, but Santa Anna had used only a portion of his men. If the Mexicans attacked in full force, the Alamo could hold out only for a short time. Travis had little doubt that Santa Anna had reached the same conclusion.

After the day's fighting, Santa Anna surveyed the Mexican lines, riding out to talk things over with his commanders. While making his rounds, the general gave directions as to where to locate artillery pieces and trenches. Slowly, the Mexicans extended their lines around the Alamo. Artillery now flanked three sides of the compound while cavalry protected the fourth. The attacking force was tightening its hold on the fort.

Later that day, Santa Anna contemplated his chances at taking the garrison. The general then sent a high-ranking messenger with orders to General Antonio Gaona, who still lagged far behind Santa Anna's army. Gaona led 1,600 troopers, and Santa Anna wanted these men at his disposal. More important, Gaona also had two large 12-pound cannon. With these, Santa Anna could reduce the Alamo walls to rubble. He was angry that Gaona had not yet arrived to reinforce his position.

Although Santa Anna had strengthened his grip on the Alamo, it was virtually impossible to make the Mexican lines impenetrable. A single messenger could still slip through, provided he was cautious. While Santa Anna now had enough men and artillery surrounding the Alamo to prevent a mass escape, the general did not want any defenders to escape. Instead, he wanted to teach all Texians a lesson. Thus, the red flag continued to fly from the San Fernando Church. There would be no quarter given to the men inside the Alamo. If the American defenders did not understand their situation, those of Mexican descent certainly did. Several Tejanos left during the night after the failed attack on the south wall.

Occasionally throughout the night, the Mexicans launched a few shells into the Alamo to prevent the defenders from resting. Buglers sporadically blared their tunes to break the silence. Mexican crews also used the darkness to their advantage, moving several of their artillery pieces closer to the fort. The Mexicans were methodically constricting the perimeter around their prey.

Travis, from the peace of his quarters, kept track of the movements of Santa Anna and the tightening grip in which the defenders found themselves. He also weighed sending Juan Seguín to deliver an urgent message to Houston. It was a difficult decision, since Juan spoke fluent Spanish and his services might be needed in the case of additional negotiations. Those same language skills, however, increased the chances that Seguín would make it through Mexican lines. Travis finally concluded that the situation demanded that Seguín go, and he dispatched the rider. Since Seguín's horse was unhealthy, the Tejano visited James Bowie late that night and borrowed a horse from the ailing defender. Seguín and another Tejano, Antonio Cruz y Arocha, headed out of the Alamo, taking the Gonzales Road. Almost immediately, a Mexican patrol confronted them. Seguín kept his composure and nonchalantly talked with the troops for a few minutes. Then, suddenly, the two riders rushed off into the darkness. The Mexicans fired shots in their direction, but the two escaped unhurt. The Alamo's plea for help was now en route.

THE CONTINUING SIEGE

As the siege went on, the Mexicans drew the encirclement tighter while the defenders resisted this effort. At daybreak on the fourth day of the siege, General Ramirez y Sesma led a small cavalry unit to the northern side of the Alamo. Defenders fired at the mounted troopers until they retreated to safety. The volunteers spent the rest of the day digging trenches under a cloudy sky in the chilly air.

Meanwhile, 95 miles east of San Antonio, Colonel Fannin prepared to send at least 300 men to relieve the Alamo. Unfortunately for the defenders within the mission compound, Fannin was anything but a decisive leader. Over the next several days, he would make a decision only to reanalyze the situation and change his mind. Each time he changed his mind, the window of opportunity to help those in the Alamo narrowed. In the end, Fannin vacillated until relieving Travis was no longer an option.

At the Alamo, nightfall offered Crockett and other marksmen the chance to wreak fear on the Mexican troops. Those foolish enough to expose themselves within 200 yards risked receiving a life-ending shot from a long rifle. Soon, the Mexicans understood the danger Crockett presented and kept their distance. One Mexican officer described the frontiersman as follows:

> A tall man, with flowing hair, was seen firing from the same place on the parapet during the entire siege. He wore a buckskin suit and a cap all of a pattern entirely different from those worn by his comrades. This man would kneel or lie down behind the low parapet, rest his long gun, and fire, and we all learned to keep a good distance when he was seen to make ready to shoot. He rarely missed his mark, and when he fired, he always rose to his feet and calmly reloaded his gun seemingly indifferent to the shots fired at him by our men. He had a strong, resonant voice and often railed at us, but as we did not understand English we could not comprehend the import of his words further than that they were defiant.[2]

Those Mexican soldiers wishing to survive watched to see if Crockett was taking aim. The Tennessee frontiersman made a name for himself among the Mexican troops during the siege.

Having recently arrived in the Mexican province of Texas, Davy Crockett joined a small band of volunteers in their effort to defend the fortress. His reputation as a noted hunter, an expert rifleman, and a talented scout preceded him.

Several times a night, Travis sent out messengers asking for reinforcements. And each night, the Mexicans continued their barrage of cannon and small-arms fire, mixed in with shouts, insults, and an occasional bugle blast. Santa Anna was determined not to let the defenders get too much rest. In addition, he prepared for Texian reinforcements. It seemed as though the Mexican soldiers never rested. The general gave orders moving the artillery still closer to the walls. The shorter distances improved accuracy, which could only help reduce the fort's defenses. Santa Anna also sent out dispatches demanding that his remaining troops redouble their efforts and get to Bexar as soon as possible.

Each morning, the Mexicans made some new attempt to move closer to the walls. Then, the rest of the day would be relatively quiet, as soldiers dug trenches ever nearer the Alamo. The nights were filled with the sounds of the Mexicans' bugles, and throughout the siege "both sides relied on their artillery to harass their opponents."[3] Day after day, the Mexican force further constricted its coils while the Texians resisted the besiegers' efforts. In this way, the siege dragged on for those inside and outside the compound.

One morning, daylight revealed a group of Mexican soldiers taking steps to interrupt the flow of water to the Alamo from the nearby ditches. The group placed timbers across one ditch about 800 yards north of the fort near an old mill. The defenders fired on the soldiers, who fled the scene, ending this attempt to cut off a necessity to the besieged volunteers.

In addition to the hazards and tedium of siege warfare, the defenders also had to face the likely outcome. Their thoughts inevitably turned to family and friends. As Crockett wrote in his journal on February 28, "Those who fight the battles experience but a small part of the privation, suffering, and anguish that follow in the train of ruthless war."[4]

For the men inside the Alamo, most days ended with neither reinforcements nor even word from the outside world. Instead, the defenders received an occasional artillery blast accompanied by Mexican bugles and small-arms fire. They did their best to get some sleep amidst the noise of war. Santa Anna understood how to lay siege effectively, and he did so methodically. Each day, the Mexican trenches edged closer to the Alamo. Mexican artillery was close enough to continually damage the walls and harass the defenders.

REINFORCEMENTS

Inside the Alamo, simple things lifted the men's spirits. Two of the most well-known defenders played a part in boosting morale: Davy Crockett and Jim Bowie. In addition to his shooting abilities, Crockett had many other talents, among which were the ability to play the fiddle and tell stories. Crockett with his fiddle and another volunteer, Scotsman John McGregor, with his bagpipes, played dueling instruments. The musical contests delighted the men who responded with "unbridled howls and whoops."[5] Crockett also told stories to the others, resulting in smiles and laughter. For the men inside the walls of the Alamo, the presence of Crockett made the siege more bearable.

James Bowie, ill and bedridden, still had the strength to encourage his comrades. When rested and coherent, the knife-fighter asked others to carry his cot outside where his presence and cheer heartened the volunteers. Despite his failing health, Bowie offered what he could to the cause of holding out against Santa Anna's troops. Bowie also had family within the walls to consider and daily he offered comforting words to his sisters-in-law, assuring them that they would be safe.

Besides the talents and character of Crockett and Bowie, the beleaguered defenders found little to lift their spirits during the siege. It appeared that the provisional government and Sam Houston had forgotten the band and their plight. The settlement of Gonzales, however, where the first armed resistance against the centralist government of Mexico had occurred the previous fall, heard the call for help and decided to act. Captain George Kimbell gathered about 30 mounted men, all volunteers, to ride to San Antonio. The group, calling itself the Gonzales Ranging Company, was ready to go to join the men inside the Alamo. John W. Smith, one of the couriers who rode out of the Alamo on the first day of the siege, served as the guide. Two other couriers from the Alamo also rode with the Gonzales Ranging Company. The small relief column arrived at the Alamo early in the morning of March 1. Although the arrival of 32 additional defenders boosted morale and Travis welcomed the extra bodies, the commander also realized that he needed far more men and supplies if the Alamo was to hold out.

"CHICKENS"

In the final days of the siege, Santa Anna met with his staff and discussed how to proceed. The general suggested an all-out assault. Several officers wanted to wait a few more days. The continuation of the siege had severely depleted the Alamo's supplies. No reinforcements for the Texians had appeared. In addition, Santa Anna was expecting the arrival of heavier cannon within a few days. The walls of the Alamo would be no defense against their firepower. Mexican artillery could batter the walls down until the defenders had no choice but to surrender. Overall, "there was simply no valid military justification for the costly attack on a stronghold bristling with cannons."[6]

General Santa Anna, however, was in no mood to wait for those cannon. He resented the defiance the defenders had already displayed and feared that such bold insolence, if left unpunished, would encourage more Texians to rise up against Mexican authority. He wanted to make an example of the rebels within the Alamo. He was also aware that two of the defenders, Davy Crockett and Jim Bowie, were well-known Americans. He worried that if Americans were allowed to enter Mexican territory and incite rebellion without consequences, the stream of such foreigners would only multiply.

Santa Anna also exhibited the arrogant attitude that the cost to the Mexican army was unimportant. Colonel Urissa, an officer on Santa Anna's staff, recalled the general's callous attitude toward the safety of his men. An officer had appealed to Santa Anna, arguing that an assault would inevitably result in the loss of many Mexican lives. As he spoke of his doubt, the general was eating and held up the leg of a chicken, saying, "What are the lives of soldiers more than of so many chickens? I tell you, the Alamo must fall, and my orders must be obeyed at all hazards. If our soldiers are driven back, the next line in their rear must force those before them forward, and compel them to scale the walls, cost what it may."[7]

His past training and experience had led him to one conclusion: The Mexicans must storm the fort. When he suggested this, he knew it would stir resistance in his officers and indeed, several voiced strong opposition to the idea. Santa Anna listened and then dismissed their concerns. Although he did not explicitly state that he intended to attack, those who knew him well understood that a frontal assault was inevitable. On March 5, Santa Anna directed his secretary (Colonel Urissa) to write out orders announcing his decision: He intended to take the Texian positions by force. The Mexicans were going to storm the Alamo.

FACING THE END

Late in the afternoon of March 5, the Mexican artillery ceased firing. After waiting to see if it was more than a temporary lull, Travis assembled the entire garrison, including the wounded, in the courtyard of the compound. He addressed them as their commander, as a colleague, as a fellow comrade-in-arms. The 26-year-old officer told them the truth: No help was coming. Travis encouraged them to be brave, said that he intended to fight to the end, and then allowed men to make their own choice. Only Louis Rose, a 50-year-old Frenchman, chose to leave. After the group dispersed, Rose took his few belongings and disappeared over the wall. He managed to walk to freedom—many later criticized him for leaving.

Travis was aware that the end was near. As he made the rounds that evening, he encouraged his men. He posted sentries outside walls. If an attack was coming, he wanted the defenders

JAMES BONHAM
(1807–1836)

The Last Man In

Of the many compelling stories of the defenders on that last night, one stands out: James Bonham, who was the last man to enter the Alamo before it fell. Born in 1807, in Edgefield, South Carolina, Bonham died defending the Alamo on March 6, 1836. The future volunteer was used to controversy. As a student at South Carolina College (later the University of South Carolina), he led a student protest objecting to the food, class attendance policy, and the institution's stance on states' rights. The college expelled him in 1824 for his radicalism.

Bonham then studied law and established his own practice in Pendleton, South Carolina. He earned a reputation as a fiery courtroom attorney. It was also in South Carolina that his views on states' rights earned him the post of colonel and command of an artillery company in Charleston during the Nullification Crisis, a question of tariffs, in which South Carolina asserted its rights as a state against the federal government led by President Andrew Jackson and the U.S. Congress.

Bonham worked with William B. Travis, a former classmate and friend, to create the Mobile Greys, a volunteer unit from New Mobile, Alabama, that supported Texian independence. As with other to have as much warning as possible. The young commander stopped for a few moments in the chapel, talking briefly with Susannah Dickinson, wife of Captain Almeron Dickinson, and their 15-month-old daughter, Angelina. Before leaving, Travis removed from his finger the gold ring with the cat's-eye stone, given to him by his fiancée, Rebecca Cummings, and tied it

Southerners, the promise of Texas proved irresistible to Bonham, who migrated there in November 1835. Upon his arrival, Bonham volunteered to aid Sam Houston without pay. Houston appointed him second lieutenant in the cavalry. He arrived at the Alamo with James Bowie on January 19, 1836. There, Bonham involved himself with many of the efforts to make Texas independent from Mexico.

Before Santa Anna laid siege to the Alamo, Travis sent Bonham to Colonel James Fannin in Goliad, seeking reinforcements. Bonham returned empty-handed on February 23, the day the siege began. Four days later, Travis again sent Bonham out to get reinforcements. He hurried to Goliad, to accentuate the Alamo's dire need for reinforcements. Fannin again rejected Travis's pleas and Bonham headed back to San Antonio. When he arrived, he saw that the Mexican force had tightened its hold on the Alamo. Bonham's orders allowed him to seek help elsewhere, but he chose to reenter the Alamo compound.

On March 3, Bonham slipped through the Mexican lines. He returned with bad news for Travis: Goliad would send no reinforcements. Three days later, the final attack on the Alamo began just before dawn. During that battle, Mexican troops killed James Butler Bonham as he fought atop the platform of the church, next to the two 12-pound cannon. The town of Bonham, Texas, was named in honor of the last man to enter the Alamo before it fell.

onto a string, which he placed around young Angelina's neck. Then Travis retired to his quarters.

The men inside the Alamo readied themselves for the night. Some slept in their bunks and some lay in their assigned positions, while others remained on duty. After the tiresome siege and Travis's moving speech, the thoughts of many turned toward home and loved ones. The brave souls remaining were well aware of the costs of their attempt to defend the Alamo.

The Fall
of the Alamo

Mexican forces began preparations for the final assault shortly after midnight on March 6. That Sunday marked the thirteenth and final day of the siege. Santa Anna divided his troops into four columns and chose his brother-in-law, General Martín Perfecto de Cos, to lead the Aldamas battalion of Mexican regulars. This column, comprised of 500 men, was to attack the west wall of the Alamo Mission. Colonel Francisco Duque, who led the second column, was to attack the north wall with the three companies of the San Luis volunteers, which included about 500 men. Ordered to spearhead the attack on the eastern wall was Colonel José María Romero, leading about 300 regulars of the Jimenez and Matamoras battalions. The fourth and final column was to attack the south gate and the wooden-stake palisade.

In addition to the four columns, about 300 Mexican cavalrymen waited in the east to cut off any escaping defenders. Santa Anna remained with a group of some 400 reserves, including the artillery units. Each soldier carried between four and six cartridges for his rifle. Each column received the tools necessary to climb and breach walls, such as scaling ladders, crowbars, and axes. Expecting hand-to-hand combat, Mexican officers ordered their men to check their equipment, especially their bayonets. There is little doubt that Santa Anna was determined to fight this battle with foot soldiers on the ground rather than simply pound the fort into submission with artillery.

THE BEGINNING OF THE END

The Mexican army waited for the order to move forward. The dark sky began to lighten on the eastern horizon as dawn approached. Shortly after 5:00 A.M., one Mexican soldier could wait no longer and cried out, "Viva Santa Anna!" Others quickly echoed the cry, and still others cried out, "Viva la republica!" until there were literally hundreds of shouting voices. The element of surprise now gone, Santa Anna ordered his bugler to sound the attack. Officers yelled "*Ariba*" (Spanish for attack) to their men, spurring the Mexican line to advance quickly toward the fort. Four columns of men descended on the small compound. The assault was underway.

Attackers and defenders alike also heard the sound of the Mexican military band as it played *Düguello*, the Spanish tune signifying no quarter (the red flag carried the same meaning). Translated, *düguello* means "to slit the throat."[1] "The Mexicans had inherited the düguello from the Spaniards, who in turn had borrowed it from the Moors."[2] The Mexican buglers and Mexican soldiers' shouts served as the only alarm for the men inside the Alamo.

When he heard the alarm, Colonel Travis bolted out of bed. Armed with a double-barreled shotgun and sword, Travis called to his slave, Joe, and the two of them quickly ran outside to the north wall. The young commander shouted, "Come on boys, the Mexicans are upon us and we'll give them Hell!"[3] Travis shouted orders and took his place on the wall. The advancing troops were already within rifle range and the defenders fired at the onrushing enemy. Texian artillery roared, spewing grapeshot into the mass of Mexican attackers. Many defenders had several loaded weapons at their place, allowing them to fire three or four times before stopping to reload. The initial salvo slowed the attack.

As the three main columns of the assault advanced from the north and east, Texian artillery ripped through their ranks. The defensive fire pushed the three columns together. Despite the withering fire, the Mexican forces continued to move forward, collecting beneath the north wall, but they found themselves unable to scale it as they could not locate the scaling ladders. Nor could they retreat, as many more advancing troops crowded toward the north wall. From above, Texians poured down small-arms fire on the trapped attackers. The position did offer one advantage, as the Mexicans' proximity to the walls meant the Texians could not aim their artillery pieces on them.

Defenders on the north wall fired their guns into the mass of men below them. After Travis fired his shotgun and paused to reload, he was struck in the forehead by a bullet. The Texian commander dropped backward and rolled down the cannon ramp. Still grasping his sword, he came to rest at the bottom. Mortally wounded, Travis remained seated on the ground as the battle continued to rage. Dazed and unable to rise, the unshakeable leader of the Alamo defenders was one of the first Americans to die in the assault. Joe, his slave, saw his master fall and die before fleeing to safety in one of the rooms of the compound. The battle was only about 15 minutes old.

At this moment, Santa Anna decided to throw his reserves into the melee. From his position, the Mexican general could

FLAGS IN AMERICA'S HISTORY

✧ THE LAST STAND AT THE ALAMO ✧

The flag that floated over the ill-fated mission fortress The Alamo, at San Antonio, in 1836, was that of the Republic of Texas, then fighting for the right to self-government. Its design was that of the Mexican flag, with the eagle, serpent and cactus replaced by the date 1824. This indicated adherence to the Texas constitution of that date, overthrown by Santa Anna, who established a dictatorship. Besieged by 4,000 troops under Santa Anna, the little garrison of 183 Americans held out 12 days under constant bombardment.

1824

From the flat roof with its thick adobe walls, the Texan sharpshooters directed a devastating fire in the defense described in the diary left by Davy Crockett, famed scout, hunter and Indian fighter whose career ended here. Finally the defenders were so weakened that, after two unsuccessful assaults, an entrance was made through sheer weight of numbers and the five lone survivors were slain. The slogan "Remember the Alamo" became a battle-cry which led to Santa Anna's destruction and the ultimate victory of the Texans.

THE ALAMO FLAG

The Texian soldiers had almost been caught totally unaware, but the defenders on the wall rallied quickly and sent a veritable shower of shots into the crowd of Mexican soldiers. The painting *Last Stand at the Alamo* depicts the last few moments of the fight. Although outnumbered and overwhelmed, the Texians fought hard and 600 Mexican soldiers were killed.

not see why and how the advance had stalled. Thus, another 400 men rushed into the chaotic struggle. As the reserves approached, they fired toward the fort, inflicting casualties on their own troops crowded together beneath the north wall. The effect of the additional push, however, forced many to try to climb the walls in any possible way. The scaling ladders finally materialized and soldiers began the arduous and deadly task of ascending the wall.

Meanwhile, Colonel Morales led his column of 100 men to the south wall. The defenders initially repulsed this column, forcing Morales and his men to fall back and regroup. As the three attacking columns bunched their attack on the south wall, defenders hurried to the north wall to reinforce the position against the large mass of troops clustered there. In so doing, the south wall was now vulnerable to the second attack by the Morales column. Facing little resistance, Morales and his men scaled the wall and seized the 18-pound cannon. Mexican troops were now inside the Alamo compound.

Susannah Dickinson waited within a small room in the church, trying to comfort her young daughter as she held the child in her arms. The sounds of fighting grew louder and closer with each passing moment. Abruptly, Galba Fuqua, a 16-year-old defender, rushed into the room. When she saw him bleeding from his mouth, Dickinson realized that a bullet had struck Fuqua's jaws. The teen tried, fruitlessly, to speak, but unable to make himself understood, he shook his head and returned to the fighting outside the church.

BREACHED

After Morales's men had secured their position on the south wall, he sent them across the courtyard to attack the defenders at the north wall from behind. At that moment, attacking troops were on the verge of breaching the walls and overwhelming the defenders. Texians faced Mexican soldiers scaling the walls and fired constantly. The first wave of Mexicans faced almost certain death as they climbed. When they reached the top, the defenders used pistols, rifles, rifle butts, knives, and bayonets; anything they could to fight off the raging horde. In the end, it was a matter of superior numbers. There were only so many defenders facing tremendous odds as increasingly more Mexicans managed to get higher up the wall. Soon, great numbers of attackers stood within the walls. The tide was turning inevitably against the defenders.

Those Texians who were able retreated into the courtyard. There they met the incoming attackers in savage hand-to-hand fighting. Mexican troops poured into the courtyard and attacked the defenders from inside the fort. As the Mexican force began breaching the north wall, General Cos maneuvered his column to the 500-foot west wall, which had only 20 to 30 volunteer defenders. They fought valiantly but lacked the firepower to prevent the attackers from scaling the wall. Several Mexicans managed to open the northern gate, allowing dozens of angry soldiers to pour through unmolested. The Mexicans were over-running the defenders. Almeron Dickinson rushed into the church and found his wife and daughter still hiding in a small room. Dickinson cried out, "Great God, Sue, the Mexicans are inside our walls!"[4] Then he rushed away to rejoin the fighting. It was the last time Susannah saw her husband alive.

Captain John Baugh ordered all who could to retreat to the long barracks, but some of the volunteers were caught out in the open by Mexican troops and even a few mounted cavalry. The attackers shot and bayoneted those unfortunate enough to be stranded in the courtyard. The remaining defenders fell back into the long barracks and readied themselves for a final defense.

At this point, a large group of volunteers scaled the wall and headed out of the Alamo. Unfortunately, Mexican cavalry waited to prevent such an escape. A group of several dozen Texians, perhaps as many as 75, met their deaths at the end of Mexican lances. One defender managed to climb deep into the underbrush where the lancers could not reach him. Unable to force him out, "it was necessary for the soldiers to shoot him where he hid."[5]

Jim Bowie lay in a room located near the low barracks, too sick to stand. Mexican soldiers battered down the door and charged in to find the famous knife-fighter lying down, but propped up and armed. Bowie fired two pistols before the incoming troops bayoneted him to death. Some claim the enraged soldiers mutilated his body with their bayonets, spilling his blood throughout the small room—a sad end for one of America's most highly reputed warriors.

THE LONG BARRACKS

During the siege, the defenders had made preparations to use the long barracks for their last stand. To buttress the defense of each doorway facing the inside of the compound, the Texians had placed an arched bulwark made of stretched cowhide and filled with dirt. Inside many of the rooms, trenches acted as barriers and foxholes. The Texians cut out holes through which they could fire and pass from room to room. The long barracks consisted of a winding maze in which the defenders intended to fight to the end.

As they moved back into the barracks, they had no time to disable their own cannon. Now the 18-pounder was used against them. Mexican troops wheeled the big gun to the building and aimed the cannon at the blockaded doorways, blasting their way into each room. Then, they wheeled the cannon up to the doorway and blasted the defenders within. Concentrated musket fire preceded a mad rush into each room, where bayonets finished the job. The attackers had the advantage of numbers and slowly, at great cost, Mexican soldiers eradicated defenders room by room.

THE DEATH OF CROCKETT

One of the most enduring and spirited debates about the Battle of the Alamo concerns the death of an American icon: Davy Crockett. How the frontiersman met his end has been the

Davy Crockett, shown with his rifle above his head, and his men kept the Mexican infantry at bay, forcing them to shift their attack further south. Once the Mexican soldiers breached the walls of the Alamo, the fight turned to hand-to-hand combat. The defenders stayed and fought to the bitter end, and the legend began to grow and eventually overshadow reality.

subject of much scholarship and controversy. Some believe he fell in front of the chapel. Several Mexican accounts, however, claim that Crockett survived the battle and was one of five or six defenders taken prisoner. These captives appeared before Santa Anna who immediately ordered their execution. Such a death for Crockett doesn't fit the celebrated and popular portrait of the frontier fighter wielding his rifle as a club against a growing number of Mexican soldiers. In 1837, a visitor to the site observed, "That Crockett fell at the Alamo is all that is known"; "by whom or how, no one can tell."[6] At least one historian believes that "too much has been made over the details of *how* David died at the Alamo."[7] Perhaps it is more important that he fell, rather than how. Indeed, historians know that Crockett fought and died at the Alamo in defense of Texas liberty. Little beyond those general facts can be confirmed or denied.

THE GRUESOME END

The Mexican troops scoured the entire Alamo compound, looking for any survivors and killed any they found. Entering the crude hospital housing the sick and wounded, soldiers quickly dispatched the helpless ones within.

The killing frenzy extended even past death. After finding and killing all the defenders, soldiers then used their bayonets and rifles to disfigure and mutilate the corpses. Yet, as Travis had predicted, the Mexicans paid dearly for their victory. Their actions immediately following the battle demonstrate the rage inflamed by the cost of victory in Mexican lives.

After holding out for 12 long days, Travis and his men managed to fight off the advancing Mexican army for about 90 minutes in the final assault. In the end, the Mexican numbers simply overwhelmed the volunteers inside the fort. By 6:30 A.M., the battle was over. Santa Anna and his Mexican force now held the Alamo.

Dead bodies littered the mission grounds. One of Santa Anna's officers exclaimed, "What a sad spectacle, that of the dead and dying! What a horror, to inspect the area and find the remains of friends."[8] Santa Anna toured the battlefield before making a speech to his troops. He addressed the victors, "lauding their courage and thanking them in the name of their country."[9] The general called the battle a great victory. Many of his officers disagreed. The dead and wounded included many of their own men. However, Santa Anna insisted the battle would serve to make a statement as to the fate of rebels against the centralist government.

THE DE LA PEÑA DIARY

What really happened to the last defenders of the Alamo? Historians offer a variety of answers to that question. Part of the problem is that the surviving eyewitnesses had different and, in many cases, limiting vantage points. Mexican accounts often differed on key points. Perhaps the most complete and controversial Mexican account is found in the diary of José Enrique De la Peña. The most contentious passage describes the death of Davy Crockett, not in the midst of a savage battle, but as a ruthless execution. The section also portrays the frontier hero as somewhat cowardly, willing to lie in order to escape with his life. Here is the De la Peña exerpt:

> Some seven men had survived the general carnage and under the protection of General Castrillón, they were brought before Santa Anna. Among them was one of great stature, well proportioned, with regular features, in whose face there was the imprint of adversity, but in whom one also noticed a degree of resignation and nobility that did him honor. He was the naturalist David Crockett, well known in North America for his unusual

Santa Anna decided to make another statement to other Texians by the way in which he treated the Alamo dead. The general ordered his men to drag the bodies of the rebels outside the Alamo. The victors gathered the remains of the vanquished at Alameda, at the road to Gonzales. The primary thoroughfare into the colonies, the Gonzales Road served as the key transportation artery into the Alamo. Most of the dead defenders had traveled into the area on this road. Now, their bodies were about to endure public humiliation next to that same road.

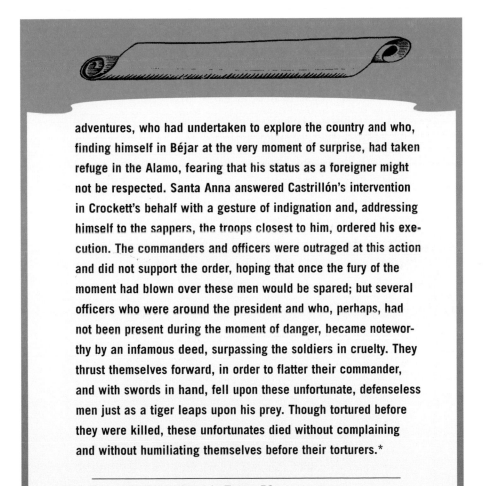

adventures, who had undertaken to explore the country and who, finding himself in Béjar at the very moment of surprise, had taken refuge in the Alamo, fearing that his status as a foreigner might not be respected. Santa Anna answered Castrillón's intervention in Crockett's behalf with a gesture of indignation and, addressing himself to the sappers, the troops closest to him, ordered his execution. The commanders and officers were outraged at this action and did not support the order, hoping that once the fury of the moment had blown over these men would be spared; but several officers who were around the president and who, perhaps, had not been present during the moment of danger, became noteworthy by an infamous deed, surpassing the soldiers in cruelty. They thrust themselves forward, in order to flatter their commander, and with swords in hand, fell upon these unfortunate, defenseless men just as a tiger leaps upon his prey. Though tortured before they were killed, these unfortunates died without complaining and without humiliating themselves before their torturers.*

*De la Peña with Santa Anna in Texas, 53.

Mexican soldiers built two pyres comprised of slain Texians, wood, kindling, and oil. The fires were lit and within minutes, the air was filled with thick smoke and the smell of burning flesh.

Francisco Antonio Ruiz, the mayor of Bexar, wrote about his role in the funeral pyre experience:

> Santa Anna, after all the Mexicans were taken out, ordered wood to be brought to burn the bodies of the Texians. He sent a company of dragoons with me to bring wood and dry branches from the neighboring forest. About 3 o'clock in the afternoon, they commenced laying the wood and dry branches, upon which a pile of dead bodies was placed; more wood was piled on them, and another pile brought, and in this manner they were all arranged in layers. Kindling wood was distributed throughout the pile, and about 5 o'clock in the evening it was lighted.[10]

A local teenager later said, "I saw an immense pillar of fire shoot up south and east of the Alamo, and dense smoke rose high into the clouds."[11] The funeral pyre smoldered for two days. A year later, Juan Seguín led a detachment of cavalry back to the Alamo where they recovered some of the ashes of the fallen. The troops paid honor to the remains by performing the rites of a military funeral.

Aftermath

The Mexicans did not kill everyone within the walls of the Alamo. One defender, Brigido Guerrero, had deserted the Mexican army in 1835. As the fighting waned, Guerrero hid. Soldiers eventually found him, but as he claimed he was merely a prisoner of the Texians, Mexican officers believed him and spared his life. Officers intervened and spared women and young children. At least two or three Tejano women, including Senora Candelaria and Bowie's sister-in-law, who had stayed inside the fort, survived. Following the battle, General Santa Anna toured the compound before offering a congratulatory speech to his men. Then he had each of the survivors brought before him. The general sat on the north end of the courtyard, drinking coffee.

Susannah Dickinson and her 15-month-old daughter, Angelina, were two of the survivors. By some accounts, Santa

Anna offered to adopt and raise Angelina as a princess, but Susannah refused him. The general persisted for a brief time, but one of his officers—Colonel Juan Almonte, who translated the conversation for the two—convinced him to drop the matter. Santa Anna then gave Susannah two pesos and a blanket before releasing her and her daughter.

William Travis's slave, Joe, also survived the attack. After seeing his master die, Joe found refuge inside one of the rooms of the fort. Upon his capture, several soldiers threatened him, but an officer ordered them to leave him alone. He was taken to General Cos, who demanded that Joe point out the body of William Travis. Standing over the lifeless body of the fallen Alamo commander, General Cos then mutilated the colonel's face and limbs with his sword.

"BUT A SMALL AFFAIR"

A Mexican force of about 6,000 soldiers had overwhelmed the Alamo and its approximately 183 defenders. Loss numbers for the Mexican army are more difficult to determine. Low estimates put the figure at 70 dead and more than 300 wounded, many of those, seriously. Others place the Mexican death toll much higher, at 1,600. Still others claim the Mexicans lost 200 to 300 men in the assault. The lower estimates seem more likely, and many of the Mexican injured died in the days and weeks following the battle. Thus, the Mexican army probably suffered up to 400 casualties (dead and wounded) in the battle. Despite the great cost, Santa Anna reportedly described the battle as "but a small affair."[1] Yet around him lay not only the dead defenders, but also many of his own men. He had indeed won the battle but at a very high cost. In taking the Alamo, the Mexican army lost many of its best troops. Nearly one-third of his men were either killed or wounded in the assault. Worse still, the Mexicans suffered "the heaviest losses among the sergeants and corporals, those essential connections between the commanders at the top and privates in the ranks."[2] The impact of

Santa Anna's costly victory became evident at the Battle of San Jacinto six and a half weeks later. Lacking accomplished officers in the middle tier of command helped the rebel Texians score a decisive victory.

Indeed, the cost of victory stunned many of Santa Anna's army and officers. One eyewitness claimed, "The gallantry of the few Texians who defended the Alamo was really wondered at by the Mexican army."[3] The same account also states, "Even the Generals were astonished at their vigorous resistance, and how dearly victory had been bought."[4]

Santa Anna dispatched a report to Mexico City in which he told of his victory at the Alamo. The general described the army's success as "a complete and glorious triumph that will render its memory imperishable."[5] Ironically, the memory of the Alamo did live on, but not in the way or for the reasons Santa Anna had envisioned. Instead, the Alamo came to symbolize bold noncompliance despite little chance of success or survival. The battle served as a call to resist, not to retreat or submit.

Santa Anna presumed that news of the fall of the Alamo would convince Texians that their cause was ill fated. Instead, word of the Alamo roused passions against Mexico. No longer were settlers content to allow Mexico to rule over them. Mexico became the enemy to all who desired freedom or a secure life in Texas. Santa Anna's actions at the Alamo worked against his larger goal of bringing Texas under control. With the general's firm order against taking prisoners and killing every defender, Texians now understood the threat of tyranny from Mexico City. Furthermore, the sacrifices made at the Alamo provided Texian leaders with the moral high ground as they sought to drive out the invading armies. In short, Santa Anna won the battle, but the way in which he won it most likely cost him the war.

Reports of the Alamo's fall spread throughout Texas, then to the United States. The news stunned the nation. One resident of Tennessee wrote years later that "adult men and women shed tears on account of the death of David Crockett. None who knew him personally did not love him; none who were familiar with his public career, that did not admire him. The whole people of the state were then, as now, proud of him."[6]

INDEPENDENCE

On March 1, 1836, the eighth day of the Alamo siege, a group of delegates convened to discuss the Texas situation. This meeting, called the Texas Constitutional Convention, was the meeting the Texas Consultation of Delegates called for when that group adjourned in mid-November 1835. On March 2, the convention declared Texas independent of Mexico. Although word of the declaration failed to reach the Alamo defenders, many are convinced that those within the fort felt that such a declaration was inevitable. Indeed, evidence suggests that those inside the Alamo believed they were fighting for independence. William Travis said it well when he wrote on March 3,

> If independence is not declared, I shall lay down my arms, and so will the men under my command. But under a flag of independence, we are ready to peril our lives a hundred times a day, and to drive away the monster who is fighting us under a blood-red flag, threatening to murder all prisoners and make Texas a waste desert.[7]

Even though the men inside the Alamo did not learn of the declaration of Texian independence, they waged a heroic battle for the cause of freedom and independence.

THE GOLIAD MASSACRE

When the Alamo fell on March 6, the force in Goliad that Travis desired found itself still commanded by the hesitant Colonel Fannin. His indecisiveness might have cost the Alamo

The Texas Declaration of Independence was of paramount importance because the Alamo was under siege while it was being written. On March 1, 1836, at the Convention of 1836, the declaration was written, reviewed, and then adopted by the delegates the following day.

defenders, but in all likelihood, Fannin's lack of certainty may have meant fewer Alamo dead, as he could not have sent enough troops to change the outcome. When he finally decided on a course of action, he often second-guessed himself and reversed course, sometimes repeatedly. For the men inside Fort Defiance, such leadership offered little hope of success. After the fall of the Alamo, the fortress at the Goliad became an obvious target for the advancing Mexican armies.

Nevertheless, Fannin continued to dawdle. A dispatch from Houston arrived on March 12, ordering Fannin to abandon Goliad. Instead of leaving immediately, he squandered valuable time trying to evacuate settlers. He also sent out two different mounted detachments, each of which General Urrea destroyed. Word of the fate of the second detachment reached Fannin on March 17, but when the inept commander finally decided to leave the fort on March 18, Mexican cavalry were already in the vicinity and briefly skirmished with an advance unit. The lead detachment returned and Fannin pondered his next move.

Fannin finally left Goliad on March 19, the rain and fog from a storm the night before covering their escape for several hours. Nonetheless, Fannin had "hesitated too long where he was."[8] He finally began his retreat "in broad daylight across open and arid terrain away from the water, instead of by foot-hills and at night."[9] Urrea was a skilled commander and took advantage of the inexperienced Fannin. After maneuvering his forces between the Texians and the closest water source, Urrea's forces caught the Texians in the open. After failing to reach some nearby trees, Fannin and his men faced the dreadful situation of being "caught in the open without natural cover and surrounded by the Mexican cavalry."[10] The beleaguered force did the best it could, forming a square and placing its cannon on the corners to provide as much cover as possible. Mexican sharpshooters inflicted wounds and deaths, one at a time. The hapless Texians fought bravely but were unable to improve the situation. Nightfall came, but with it came a drenching rainstorm that spoiled their remaining gunpowder. The same night, Urrea's reinforcements arrived, bringing with them a howitzer. Fannin realized that the Mexican force surrounded his men. Worse still, Fannin's men lacked water. Many under his command already felt the effects of severe thirst. Soon, the lack of water would prevent the Texians from firing their cannon. Fannin and his officers had decided to fight at least one more day, but the deteriorating conditions made such a course of action impossible. After Urrea's forces fired just a few rounds the next morning, the surrounded Texians waved a white flag and "Fannin requested conditional surrender."[11] Urrea lacked the authority to negotiate terms and refused anything less than unconditional surrender. The Mexican commander did pledge to send Fannin's requests to Santa Anna. Still, Fannin unconditionally surrendered to Urrea because he realized that he and his men were "outnumbered, out of water, with no hope of succor from the colonies."[12]

Fannin and his men placed themselves at the mercy of General Urrea, who probably was aware of what doom awaited the captured Texians. The captives marched back to Goliad, entering the very fort they had abandoned just days earlier. Urrea left Goliad, placing Colonel Jose Nicolas de la Portilla in charge. True to his word, Urrea also wrote Santa Anna, asking that the prisoners receive mercy. Santa Anna, still incensed over the whole rebellious affair, sent unmistakable orders—he sent three copies of the same orders for the prisoners' execution, which reached Colonel Portilla on Saturday evening, March 26.

The next morning was Palm Sunday. At approximately 8:00 A.M., soldiers marched the 342 Texians out of Fort Defiance in three separate columns to meet their destiny. At the chosen site, a few hundred yards from the fort, soldiers halted the columns. Then, without warning, the *soldados* opened fire on the defenseless prisoners. Those fortunate enough to survive the barrage faced the lances of Mexican cavalry. Only 28 Texians managed to escape. The wounded still inside the fort met their end while they lay helpless in their beds. Portilla brought Colonel Fannin to the center of the compound and placed the injured man in a chair. After learning the fate of his men, Fannin faced a Mexican firing squad, still seated in a chair. Then, as Santa Anna had ordered after the fall of the Alamo, Mexican soldiers heaped the dead into stacks with wood and burned the bodies. The Goliad dead were now martyrs as were their Alamo comrades.

SAN JACINTO

News of the Alamo's fall "brought instant panic."[13] Residents in Gonzales did their best to leave immediately. After they vacated Gonzales, Houston and his army burned it to the ground, determined to leave nothing of value for the enemy. Houston knew he faced a much larger Mexican force, an army of at least 3,000 men. The Texians had fewer than 400 and limited resources. For such a large force, Santa Anna's army also moved quickly, covering about 25 miles a day. To accomplish this, the Mexicans needed grass for their horses. Houston initiated a policy of leaving no provisions behind for the enemy. Soon, Texians set even the grass fields ablaze to hinder the Mexican advance. Apparently, Houston learned lessons from the loss at the Alamo. The Texian leader announced that their forces "must not be shut up in forts, where they can neither be provided with men nor provisions."[14] If there were to be another battle, it would take place in the open.

Houston continued to retreat to the east and, as he retreated, he managed to attract more volunteers to the cause. Yet many in the provisional government believed Houston was unwilling to engage the enemy. Out of concern for their safety, in mid-March, government officials left the small settlement of Washington, located on the Brazos River, and reassembled in

Galveston. Thousands of terrified settlers fled as Santa Anna's army continued to pursue Houston's force. Many criticized the commanding officer, accusing him of cowardice. The president of the provisional government, David G. Burnet, disparaged Houston in a letter, writing, "Sir. The enemy is laughing you to scorn. You must fight them. You must retreat no further. The country expects you to fight. The salvation of the country depends on your doing so."[15] Houston, however, wanted to draw the enemy deep within Texas territory, further removing the advancing army from the supply depot in Bexar. Santa Anna had employed a three-column thrust in which he hoped to crush Houston's force. The long Texian retreat distracted Santa Anna, who sent one of his columns after the provisional government and another to protect his ever-lengthening supply lines. The Mexican president commanded the third and final column and continued to trail the Texian force. Soon, Houston turned southeast, bringing the two armies closer together. Finally, on April 20, the forces camped close together near Lynch's Ferry. The two sides engaged in light skirmishing on April 20, but both commanders seemed content to wait. Houston, many griped, was afraid to fight. Santa Anna knew that each passing moment meant additional reinforcements.

Houston and his force set up camp near the confluence of the Buffalo Bayou into the San Jacinto River. Although Houston was unable to retreat, it was an excellent position that offered him the choice of natural defenses or advantages if he chose to advance. Many of the Texians lacked any military training, but were anxious to engage the enemy. Houston seemed to know that "if he gave them no option but to win or die, he knew they would acquit themselves well."[16] When they first arrived, the Texians outnumbered the Mexican army. However, Houston continued to wait. Less than a mile south and east of the Texian position, the Mexican army set up camp. Both armies were now situated within the same bend of the San Jacinto River and could cross neither the San Jacinto River nor the Buffalo Bayou. The site marked the location of the decisive battle in the struggle for Texas independence from Mexico.

On the morning of April 21, both sides waited for the other army to attack. Neither side did. Houston now had about 900 men, while the Mexican force numbered about 1,500. Houston seemed content to rest, while Santa Anna appeared willing to let more reinforcements arrive. Houston ordered the destruction of Vince's Bridge, located several miles to the west. In so doing, neither army could readily escape. While the Mexican troops enjoyed their afternoon siesta, the Texians formed their lines and quietly made their way toward the enemy. Moving deliberately to maintain their lines, at about four thirty in the afternoon, the Texians appeared out of the trees within a few hundred yards of the Mexican line. The battle was about to begin.

REMEMBER THE ALAMO!

Finally, the Texians attacked. Holding their fire, Houston's men managed to close the gap between the two sides, advancing to within 300 yards or less before the Mexicans sounded the alarm. By then, it was too late. The enraged Texians shouted, "Remember the Alamo" and "Remember Goliad" as they stormed the enemy positions. Now it was the Texians who refused to give quarter, striking down many soldiers who attempted to surrender. The battle was brief, but intense. In 18 minutes of fighting, the Texians routed the Mexican force. Before the day ended, the Texians had killed some 630 Mexican soldiers while wounding 208 and capturing another 730. The victors lost 9 killed and about 30 wounded in the battle. The Texians won an overwhelming victory at San Jacinto.

As for the commanders, Houston was wounded in the ankle while Santa Anna escaped. The next day, a patrol happened upon him and captured the general. No longer wearing his flashy uniform, the Texians believed him to be an ordinary soldier until other Mexican captives began referring to him as

The captive Santa Anna is brought before Gen. Sam Houston April 22, 1836, the day after the great Texas victory at San Jacinto.

Following his success at the Alamo, General Santa Anna became overly confident. He neglected to post guards and was resting when he was taken prisoner by Sam Houston and his soldiers at San Jacinto. Santa Anna signed the treaty declaring Texas independent shortly thereafter. In this painting, Santa Anna is brought to the wounded General Sam Houston after he is captured by Houston's soldiers.

"El Presidente." The charade ended and Santa Anna identified himself. Officers brought the captive Mexican leader before Houston.

The victorious Texian general lay beneath a large oak tree, still suffering from the combat injury to his ankle. Remembering the Alamo and Goliad, many wanted Houston to execute the Mexican president. Houston believed, however, that Santa Anna was more valuable alive than dead. In return for sparing his life, Houston demanded that Santa Anna end the war and guarantee Texas independence. Three and a half weeks later, on May 14, Santa Anna signed the Treaty of Velasco. Under this pact, Santa Anna consented to withdraw all Mexican troops from Texas. Texas officials agreed to grant safe passage for Santa Anna back to Mexico in exchange for the general's support for independence. Despite Mexican clamoring and denials, the

THE OTHER TREATY OF VELASCO

When Santa Anna signed the Treaty of Velasco, he actually signed two separate agreements, one of which remained secret for many years. The private treaty included six articles intended to ensure Texas independence. Despite the pledge made in the public treaty, Texas held Santa Anna as a prisoner of war for several months rather than send him immediately to Mexico. During his captivity, the Mexican government removed him from power and refused to acknowledge any agreement he might have signed.

Later, Texas officials transferred the deposed leader to Washington, D.C., where he met President Andrew Jackson. The United States transported Santa Anna to Mexico in February 1837. The discredited ex-leader was received with hostility upon his return. Mexico refused to recognize the independence of Texas, but the young republic strengthened its government and began seeking annexation by the United States, virtually guaranteeing its sovereignty. The issue of slavery prevented U.S. annexation until 1845. Mexico refused to accept the loss of Texas, however, until it signed the Treaty of Guadalupe Hidalgo in 1848, which ended the Mexican-American War. Below is a translation of the first five articles of the secret Treaty of Velasco:

ARTICLE 1
He [Santa Anna] will not take up arms nor cause them to be taken up, against the people of Texas during the present war of Independence.

Texas Revolution was over. The cause for which the men of the Alamo had fought and died was now a reality. Texas was independent of Mexico.

ARTICLE 2

He will give his orders that, in the shortest time, the Mexican troops may leave the territory of Texas.

ARTICLE 3

He will so prepare matters in the cabinet of Mexico that the mission that may be sent thither by the government of Texas may be well received, and that by means of negotiations all differences may be settled, and the independence that has been declared by the convention may be acknowledged.

ARTICLE 4

A treaty of commerce, amity and limits will be established between Mexico and Texas, the territory of the latter not to extend beyond the Rio Bravo del Norte.

ARTICLE 5

The present return of General Santa Anna to Vera Cruz being indispensable for the purpose of effecting his solemn engagements, the government of Texas will provide for his immediate embarkation for said port.*

*Texas State Historical Society. Documents of Texas History, 2002. Available online at http://www.tea.state.tx.us/ssc/primary_resources/pdf/texas/Treaties_of_Velasco.pdf.

The Alamo's
Place in History

The role of the Alamo's fall in the Texas Revolution is significant. The courageous stand by the defenders of the Alamo helped inspire other Texians to go on with the fight. After winning independence from Mexico in May 1836, the continuing influence of American ideas and attitudes on the future of Texas is evident. The new republic voted in favor of joining the Union in September of 1836. Many believed it was the fate of Texas to become part of the United States. Given the existence of many American-like customs and fixtures of government in Texas, the new nation exhibited some of the trademark characteristics of Manifest Destiny, specifically "ideology and institutions."[1] The development of the Republic of Texas included protecting the unique American aspects of individual rights, self-governance, and religious freedom—each of which the centralist government of Mexico had threatened.

Although the slavery issue sank early attempts to incorporate Texas into the United States, the eventual success of that goal was never in question. The similarities between the principles of Texas and the United States formed a strong bond and repeatedly raised the question of annexation after the initial rebuff by the United States in 1836–1837.

THE ALAMO AFTER THE BATTLE

Six years after the battle, in 1842, the Texas Army returned the Alamo to the Roman Catholic Church. Texas entered the United States in 1845 and the United States Army rented the Alamo as a storage depot for supplies two years later. Since the building was in ruins, the army repaired the stone chapel and made many improvements. Along with the repairs, in 1849 the army added the familiar scroll that sits atop the entrance. In the same year, it also built the chapel roof.

When Abraham Lincoln won the election of 1860, Texas joined other Southern states and seceded from the Union on February 1, 1861. After the Civil War broke out, Texians forced the federal troops stationed within the Alamo to surrender. A local military force, the Alamo City Guards, held the Alamo without incident until the end of the war. Control of the facility again fell to the U.S. Army.

It was not until 1876 that the U.S. Army left the Alamo. Honore Grenet, a local merchant, purchased the non-church property and opened a general store in the long barracks. Grenet also rented the chapel from the Catholic Church for storage. In 1883, the Catholic Church sold the chapel for $20,000 to the state of Texas, which then gave the chapel to the city of San Antonio. Two years later, Honore Grenet died, and the Hugo & Schmetzer department store purchased the long barracks, which it operated until it decided to sell the property in 1903 for $75,000. At this point, the San Antonio chapter of the Daughters of the Republic of Texas, founded in 1891 to preserve Texas history, began to raise funds for the purchase. Its efforts fell short, even with the involvement of Adina de Zavala, a granddaughter of the first vice president of the Republic of Texas, Lorenzo de Zavala. However, in 1905, the granddaughter of two San Jacinto veterans, Clara Driscoll, stepped forward with a remarkable solution: an interest-free loan of $65,000 to the Daughters of the Republic of Texas to purchase the property for preservation. The Texas State Legislature repaid Driscoll's loan and then gave the Alamo to the Daughters of the Republic of Texas. In 1960, the federal government proclaimed the Alamo a national landmark.

THE ALAMO'S LEGACY

Today, the Alamo grounds cover 4.2 acres. The Alamo is believed to be the most visited tourist site in the state of Texas, boasting 2.5 million annual visitors. It also serves as the center of the San Antonio business district. But the Alamo is more than a tourist attraction—it is the cornerstone of Texas history. Given its unique birth and its struggle to gain independence, Texas is unlike any other U.S. state. The founding of Texas more closely resembles the founding of the United States than it does that of any other individual state.

In short, Texas has its own revolution story, its own heroes, villains, and martyrs. The struggle of Texas to gain independence from Mexico was expressed in the language and ideals passed down from the American fight for independence from Great Britain, which had occurred just a generation before the Texas Revolution. The Alamo is the central piece of the revolutionary history of the state of Texas. The grounds are a memorial to the sacrifice of the brave defenders who lost their lives there on March 6, 1836. The compound is a museum that tells the story of the siege and storming of the Alamo.

Today, the mission grounds serve as a constant reminder of the great struggle that took place there. The Daughters of

As the Mexican army retreated from Texas, they burned the palisade that Davy Crockett defended and tore down many of the building's walls. The Alamo church building remains standing and has been designated an official Texas state shrine. Today the Daughters of the Republic of Texas are the official caretakers.

the Texas Revolution refer to the Alamo church as the "shrine" that denotes the site as a place of pilgrimage and reverence. Visitors entering the church are greeted by a bronze plaque, which reads:

> *Be silent, friend*
> *Here heroes died*
> *To pave the way*
> *For other men*

The site is indeed a shrine, as visitors are expected to show their respect by speaking in whispers, removing their hats, and appreciating the building as a memorial to the fallen.

In military terms, Texians won the Texas Revolution at San Jacinto when they overwhelmingly defeated the Mexican army. The capture of Santa Anna the day after San Jacinto secured political independence for Texas. The execution of the Goliad defenders gave the Texians the moral authority to stand against the Centralists of Mexico City. And the sacrifices made at the Alamo gave the Texians a reason to unite against Mexican tyranny as shown by Santa Anna's cruelty in offering no quarter

WILLIAM B. TRAVIS
(1809–1836)

Travis's Bones

William B. Travis, the young and courageous commander of the Alamo, sent several communiqués out of the fort during the siege. Many of these show the bravado of a man facing his own death. Other messages refer to the struggle for independence in which the Texians found themselves. Almost all of the letters asked for help for the men besieged within the Alamo. Two of his letters offer insight into how Travis viewed the siege and battle. In one, Travis wrote Sam Houston begging for more troops and describing the advancing siege: "Our numbers are few, and the enemy still continues to approximate his works to ours. I have every reason to apprehend an attack from his whole force very soon; but I shall hold out to the last extremity, hoping to receive reinforcements in a day or two. Do hasten on aid to me as rapidly as possible; as from the superior numbers of our enemy, it will be impossible for us to hold them out much longer. If they overpower us, we fall a sacrifice at the shrine (mercy) to the defenders. The Alamo, though "a small affair" to some, was the catalyst for Texas independence.

Today, the cry "Remember the Alamo" signifies the Texan and American spirit of resolute purpose no matter the cost. The battle remains a symbol of defiance against tyranny, remembrance of courage in the face of overwhelming odds, and a shrine for the Texan struggle for independence. The Alamo church still stands, serving as a timeless memorial to the struggle that took place there in 1836. Perhaps more important, the Alamo continues to proclaim the value and price of freedom. Remember the Alamo!

of our country, and we hope posterity and our country will do our memory justice. Give me help, oh my country! Victory or death!"*

And, in one of his final letters, Travis spoke of fighting for independence and recognized that the small garrison could not hold out indefinitely and faced almost certain death. Then, he rebuked his fellow Texians for failing to relieve the Alamo. Travis writes of the day when he will die, a martyr for the cause of freedom and independence from Mexico and a reminder of Texian negligence. Here is a passage from that letter: "I shall have to fight the enemy on his own terms; yet I am ready to do it, and if my countrymen do not rally to my relief, I am determined to perish in the defence [sic] of this place, and my bones shall reproach my country for her neglect."**
He ended the letter, "My respects to all friends, and confusion to all enemies. God bless you."***

*Hansen, The Alamo Reader, 34.
**Ibid, 37–38.
***Ibid, 38.

CHRONOLOGY

1519   Spanish explorer Alonso Alvarez de Piñeda becomes the first European to map the Texas coastline.

1528   Cabeza de Vaca lands on Galveston Island.

1691   First Spanish expedition visits the San Antonio area.

1718   Mission San Antonio de Valero is founded next to San Antonio River.

1724   Construction begins on chapel located on site of the Alamo.

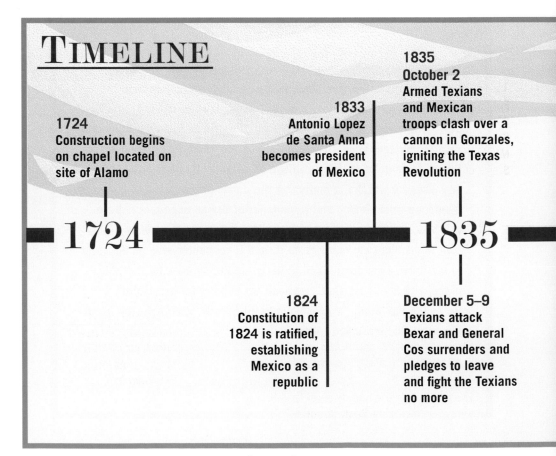

TIMELINE

1724
Construction begins on chapel located on site of Alamo

1833
Antonio Lopez de Santa Anna becomes president of Mexico

1835
October 2
Armed Texians and Mexican troops clash over a cannon in Gonzales, igniting the Texas Revolution

1724

1835

1824
Constitution of 1824 is ratified, establishing Mexico as a republic

December 5–9
Texians attack Bexar and General Cos surrenders and pledges to leave and fight the Texians no more

1793   Catholic Church abandons the mission.

1803   Spain stations a garrison at the Alamo.

1810   Mexican War of Independence begins.

1820   Moses Austin receives appointment as *empresario*, allowing him to recruit settlers to colonize Texas.

1821   Mexico gains independence from Spain.

1822   Agustin de Iturbide is declared emperor of Mexico.

1824   Constitution of 1824 is ratified, establishing Mexico as a republic.

1833   Antonio Lopez de Santa Anna becomes president of Mexico.

1836
February 23
Santa Anna reaches San Antonio; the Mexicans begin the Siege of the Alamo

March 2
Texas declares its independence from Mexico
March 6
Santa Anna's army storms the Alamo, taking no prisoners

May 14
Santa Anna signs the Treaties of Velasco, guaranteeing independence; Texas becomes an independent republic

1836   1846

April 21
Sam Houston and his forces overwhelmingly defeat the Mexican army at the Battle of San Jacinto
April 22
Texians troops capture Antonio Lopez de Santa Anna

1846
Texas enters the Union as the twenty-eighth state; the Mexican-American War begins

1834   President Santa Anna abolishes the Constitution of 1824 and establishes a centralized government in which he holds virtually all the power.

1835   **October 2** Armed Texians and Mexican troops clash over a cannon in Gonzales, igniting the Texas Revolution.

October 28 In the first major clash of the war, James Bowie leads 92 Texians against a force of 400 Mexicans in the Battle of Concepción.

November Texians surround and lay siege to a Mexican army led by General Cos in San Antonio de Bexar.

December 5–9 Texians attack Bexar and General Cos surrenders and pledges to leave and fight the Texians no more.

1836   **February 16** Leading a large army northward, Santa Anna crosses the Rio Grande.

February 23 Santa Anna reaches San Antonio; the Mexicans begin the Siege of the Alamo.

March 2 Texas declares its independence from Mexico.

March 6 Santa Anna's army storms the Alamo, taking no prisoners.

March 11 Sam Houston arrives in Gonzales, taking command of the Alamo relief force.

March 13 One of the few survivors, Susannah Dickinson (with her 15-month-old daughter), arrives in Gonzales bringing word of the Alamo's defeat.

March 27 Mexican troops ruthlessly execute James Fannin and about 340 of his men in Goliad, while only 28 escape.

April 21 Sam Houston and his forces overwhelmingly defeat the Mexican army at the Battle of San Jacinto.

April 22 Texian troops capture Antonio Lopez de Santa Anna.

May 14 Santa Anna signs the Treaties of Velasco, guaranteeing independence; Texas becomes an independent republic.

1846   Texas enters the Union as the twenty-eighth state; the Mexican-American War begins.

1848   Treaty of Guadalupe-Hidalgo ends the Mexican-American War.

1861   The Confederate army occupies the Alamo, remaining there throughout the Civil War.

1883   The state of Texas purchases the Alamo church.

1904   Clara Driscoll purchases the Alamo site.

1905   Clara Driscoll gives the Alamo site to Texas.

NOTES

CHAPTER 1

1. Lon Tinkle, *13 Days to Glory: The Siege of the Alamo*. New York: McGraw-Hill Book Company, Inc., 1958, 181.
2. Todd Hansen, ed., *The Alamo Reader: A Study in History*. Mechanicsburg, Pa.: Stackpole Books, 2003, 247.
3. Tinkle, *13 Days to Glory*, 182.
4. Alan C. Huffines, *Blood of Noble Men: The Alamo Siege and Battle*. Austin: Eakin Press, 1999, 130.
5. Walter Lord, *A Time to Stand: The Epic of the Alamo*. New York: Harper & Row, Publishers, 1961, 204.

CHAPTER 2

1. Albert A. Nofi, *The Alamo and the Texas War of Independence September 30, 1835 to April 21, 1836: Heroes, Myths, and History*. New York: De Capo Press, 1994, 15.
2. Alexis de Tocqueville, *American Institutions*. Henry Reeve, esq. translator. Boston: Sever, Francis, and Co., 1870, 554–555.

CHAPTER 3

1. Frederick Merk, *Manifest Destiny and Mission in American History: A Reinterpretation*. New York: Alfred A. Knopf, 1963, 24.
2. William Earl Weeks, *Building the Continental Empire: American Expansion from the Revolution to the Civil War*. Chicago: Ivan R. Dee, Inc., 1996, 61.
3. http://etext.virginia.edu/jefferson/grizzard/johnson/johnson13.html.
4. Hoyt, *The Alamo*, 64.
5. Thom Hatch, *Encyclopedia of the Alamo and the Texas Revolution*. Jefferson, N.C.: McFarland & Company, Inc., Publishers, 1999, 145.
6. Quoted in Thomas Ricks Lindley, *Alamo Traces: New Evidences and New Conclusions*. Lanham, Md.: Republic of Texas Press, 2003, 13.
7. Quoted in ibid.
8. Quoted in Todd Hansen, ed., *The Alamo Reader: A Study in History*. Mechanicsburg, Pa.: Stackpole Books, 2003, 21.
9. Hoyt, *The Alamo*, 69.
10. Quoted in Lindley, *Alamo Traces*, 13.
11. Ibid.
12. Quoted in John B. Shackford, ed., *David Crockett: The Man and the Legend*. Chapel Hill: The University of North Carolina Press, 1956, 226.

CHAPTER 4

1. J.R. Edmondson, *The Alamo Story: From History to Current Conflicts*. Plano, Tex.: Republic of Texas Press, 2000, 84–85.
2. Clifford Hopewell, *James Bowie, Texas Fighting Man: A Biography*. Austin: Eakin Press, 1994, 93.

3. Quoted in Stephen Hardin, *The Alamo 1836: Santa Anna's Texas Campaign*. Westport, Conn.: Praeger Publishers, 2004, 32.
4. Ibid.
5. Shackford, *David Crockett*, 8.
6. Ibid., 11.
7. Ibid., 212.
8. William C. Davis, *Three Roads to the Alamo: The Lives and Fortunes of David Crockett, James Bowie, and William Barret Travis*. New York: Harper Collins Publishers, 1998, 408.
9. Shackford, *David Crockett*, 216.
10. Ibid., 216.
11. Davis, *Three Roads to the Alamo*, 417.

CHAPTER 5

1. Carlos E. Castañeda, ed., *The Mexican Side of the Texan Revolution*. Washington, D.C.: Documentary Publications, 1971, 12–13.
2. Hansen, *The Alamo Reader*, 331.
3. Ibid., 331.
4. Shane Mountjoy, *Francisco Coronado and the Seven Cities of Gold*. Philadelphia: Chelsea House Publishers, 2006, 19.
5. http://www.thealamo.org/William_R._Carey_Letter.htm
6. Hatch, *Encyclopedia of the Alamo*, 14.
7. Richard Bruce Winders, *Sacrificed at the Alamo: Tragedy and Triumph in the Texas Revolution*. Abilene, Tex.: State House, 2004, 115.
8. Ibid., 117.
9. Ibid., 86.
10. Ibid.
11. Nofi, *The Alamo and the Texas War of Independence*, 63.

12. Hansen, *The Alamo Reader*, 28.
13. Hatch, *Encyclopedia of the Alamo*, 20.
14. Ibid.
15. Quoted in Davis, *Three Roads to the Alamo*, 537.

CHAPTER 6

1. Davis, *Three Roads to the Alamo*, 544.
2. Quoted in Hatch, *Encyclopedia of the Alamo*, 26–27.
3. Winders, *Sacrificed at the Alamo*, 118.
4. Richard Penn Smith, *On to the Alamo: Colonel Crockett's Exploits and Adventures in Texas*. New York: Penguin Classics, 2003, 114.
5. Hatch, *Encyclopedia of the Alamo*, 28.
6. http://www.tshaonline.org/handbook/online/articles/AA/qea2.html
7. Hansen, *The Alamo Reader*, 485.

CHAPTER 7

1. Huffines, *Blood of Noble Men: The Alamo Siege and Battle*. Austin: Eakin Press, 1999, 45.
2. Robert A. Calvert and Arnoldo De León, *The History of Texas*. Arlington Heights, Ill.: Harlan Davidson, Inc., 1990, 68.
3. Hardin, *The Alamo 1836*, 37.
4. Lord, *A Time to Stand*, 160.
5. Quoted in Bill Groneman, *Eyewitness to the Alamo*. Plano, Tex.: Republic of Texas Press, 1996, 76.
6. Hardin, *The Alamo 1836*, 48.
7. Shackford, *David Crockett*, 238.
8. José Enrique De la Peña (translated by Carmen Perry), *With*

Santa Anna in Texas: A Personal Narrative of the Revolution. College Station: Texas A & M University Press, 1975, 52.

9. Hansen, *The Alamo Reader*, 427.

10. Quoted in Groneman, *Eyewitness to the Alamo*, 59.

11. Hoyt, *The Alamo*, 126.

CHAPTER 8

1. Hoyt, *The Alamo*, 125.

2. Calvert and De León, *The History of Texas*, 69.

3. Quoted in Groneman, *Eyewitness to the Alamo*, 59.

4. Quoted in Ibid., 60.

5. Paul Robert Walker, *Remember the Alamo: Texians, Tejanos, and Mexicans Tell Their Stories.* Washington, D.C.: National Geographic, 2007, 54.

6. Shackford, *David Crockett*, 238.

7. Quoted in Lindley, *Alamo Traces*, 309.

8. Shackford, *David Crockett*, 225.

9. Ibid.

10. Hardin, *The Alamo 1836*, 64.

11. Alan C. Huffines, *The Texas War of Independence 1835–1836: From Outbreak to the Alamo to San Jacinto.* New York: Osprey Publishing, 2005, 53.

12. Ibid.

13. Hoyt, *The Alamo*, 129.

14. Ibid., 130.

15. Quoted in Ibid., 143.

16. Nofi, *The Alamo and the Texas War of Independence*, 150–151.

CHAPTER 9

1. Stuart, *United States Expansionism and British North America*, 85.

BIBLIOGRAPHY

Calvert, Robert A. and Arnoldo De León. *The History of Texas.* Arlington Heights, Ill.: Harlan Davidson, Inc., 1990.

Castañeda, Carlos E., ed. *The Mexican Side of the Texan Revolution.* Washington, D.C.: Documentary Publications, 1971.

Davis, William C. *Three Roads to the Alamo: The Lives and Fortunes of David Crockett, James Bowie, and William Barret Travis.* New York: HarperCollins Publishers, 1998.

De la Peña, José Enrique, translated by Carmen Perry. *With Santa Anna in Texas: A Personal Narrative of the Revolution.* College Station: Texas A & M University Press, 1975.

Groneman, Bill. *Eyewitness to the Alamo.* Plano, Tex.: Republic of Texas Press, 1996.

Hansen, Todd, ed. *The Alamo Reader: A Study in History.* Mechanicsburg, Pa.: Stackpole Books, 2003.

Hardin, Stephen. *The Alamo 1836: Santa Anna's Texas Campaign.* Westport, Conn.: Praeger Publishers, 2004.

Hatch, Thom. *Encyclopedia of the Alamo and the Texas Revolution.* Jefferson, N.C.: McFarland & Company, Inc., Publishers, 1999.

Hoyt, Edwin P. *The Alamo: An Illustrated History.* Dallas: Taylor Publishing Company, 1999.

Huffines, Alan C. *Blood of Noble Men: The Alamo Siege and Battle.* Austin: Eakin Press, 1999.

———. *The Texas War of Independence 1835–1836: From Outbreak to the Alamo to San Jacinto.* New York: Osprey Publishing, 2005.

Lindley, Thomas Ricks. *Alamo Traces: New Evidences and New Conclusions.* Lanham, Md.: Republic of Texas Press, 2003.

Mountjoy, Shane. *Francisco Coronado and the Seven Cities of Gold.* Philadelphia: Chelsea House Publishers, 2006.

Nofi, Albert A. *The Alamo and the Texas War of Independence September 30, 1835 to April 21, 1836: Heroes, Myths, and History.* New York: Da Capo Press, 1994.

Shackford, John B., ed. *David Crockett: The Man and the Legend.* Chapel Hill: The University of North Carolina Press, 1956.

Smith, Richard Penn. *On to the Alamo: Colonel Crockett's Exploits and Adventures in Texas.* New York: Penguin Classics, 2003.

Tinkle, Lon. *13 Days to Glory: The Siege of the Alamo.* New York: McGraw-Hill Book Company, 1958.

Tocqueville, Alexis de, Henry Reeve, esq. translator. *American Institutions.* Boston: Sever, Francis, and Co., 1870.

Walker, Paul Robert. *Remember the Alamo: Texians, Tejanos, and Mexicans Tell Their Stories.* Washington, D.C.: National Geographic, 2007.

Weeks, William Earl. *Building the Continental Empire: American Expansion from the Revolution to the Civil War.* Chicago: Ivan R. Dee, 1996.

Winders, Richard Bruce. *Sacrificed at the Alamo: Tragedy and Triumph in the Texas Revolution.* Abilene, Tex.: State House, 2004.

WEB SITES

The Battle of San Jacinto and the San Jacinto Campaign

http://www.tamu.edu/ccbn/dewitt/batsanjacinto.htm

The Constitution of the Mexican United States

http://www.constitution.org/cons/mexico/constit1824.htm

Letters from the Alamo

http://www.thealamo.org/William_R._Carey_Letter.htm

San Antonio Living History Association

http://www.sanantoniolivinghistory.org/

FURTHER READING

Baugh, Virgil E. *Rendezvous at the Alamo: Highlights in the Lives of Bowie, Crockett, and Travis.* Lincoln: University of Nebraska Press, 1985.

Blakely, Mike, and Mary Elizabeth Goldman, eds. *Forever Texas: Texas, the Way Those Who Lived It Wrote It.* New York: Forge Books, 2001.

Chariton, Wallace O. *Exploring the Alamo Legends.* Plano, Tex.: Wordware Publishing, 1992.

Edmondson, J.R. *The Alamo Story: From History to Current Conflicts.* Plano, Tex.: Republic of Texas Press, 2000.

Groneman, Bill. *Alamo Defenders: A Genealogy: The People and Their Words.* Austin: Eakin Press, 1990.

Hopewell, Clifford. *James Bowie, Texas Fighting Man: A Biography.* Austin: Eakin Press, 1994.

Jenkins, John H., ed. *The Papers of the Texas Revolution, 1835–1836*, 10 vols. Austin: Presidial Press, 1973.

Johnson, Frank W., *A History of Texas and Texians*, 5 vols. Edited by Eugene C. Barker. Chicago and New York: American Historical Association, 1914.

Levy, Janey. *The Alamo: A Primary Source History of the Legendary Texas Mission.* New York: The Rosen Publishing Group, 2003.

Manchaca, Martha. *Recovering History, Constructing Race: The Indian, Black, and White Roots of Mexican Americans.* Austin: University of Texas Press, 2001.

Matovina, Timothy M. *The Alamo Remembered: Tejano Accounts and Perspectives.* Austin: University of Texas Press, 1995.

McAlister, George A. *Alamo: The Price of Freedom.* San Antonio: Docutex, 1988.

McDonald, Archie P. *Travis.* Austin: Jenkins Publishing Co., 1976.

Moore, Stephen L. *Eighteen Minutes: The Battle of San Jacinto and the Texas Independence Campaign.* Dallas: Republic of Texas Press, 2004.

Petite, Mary Deborah. *1836: Facts About the Alamo and the Texas War for Independence.* Cambridge, Mass.: Da Capo Press, 1999.

Potter, Reuben Marmaduke. *The Fall of the Alamo, A Reminiscence of the Revolution of Texas.* Edited by Charles Grosvenor. Hillsdale, N.J.: Otterden Press, 1977.

Ragsdale, Crystal Sasse. *The Women and Children of the Alamo.* Austin: State House Press, 1994.

Roberts, Randy, and James S. Olson. *A Line in the Sand: The Alamo in Blood and Memory.* New York: The Free Press, 2002.

Warren, Robert Penn. *Remember the Alamo!* Eau Claire, Wis.: E.M. Hale and Company, 1958.

WEB SITES

Daughters of the Republic of Texas Library
http://www.drtl.org/

PBS-American Experience: Remember the Alamo
http://www.pbs.org/wgbh/amex/alamo/

PBS-New Perspectives on the West
http://www.pbs.org/weta/thewest/program/episodes/two/tejas.htm

San Jacinto Museum of History

http://www.sanjacinto-museum.org/

Texas Military Forces Museum

http://www.texasmilitaryforcesmuseum.org/

PHOTO CREDITS

INDEX

About the Author

DR. SHANE MOUNTJOY resides in York, Nebraska, where he is associate professor of history and dean of students at York College. Recognized by his peers and students as an outstanding teacher, Professor Mountjoy insists he is still just a student at heart. He has earned degrees from York College, Lubbock Christian University, the University of Nebraska, and the University of Missouri. He and his wife home-school their four daughters, Macy, Karlie, Ainsley, and Tessa. He is the author of several books, including *Manifest Destiny*, also in the MILESTONES OF AMERICAN HISTORY series.